Paolo
Uccello

THE ROUT OF SAN ROMANO. *Detail of Plate 51*

JOHN POPE-HENNESSY

Paolo Uccello

COMPLETE EDITION

PHAIDON *London & New York*

ALL RIGHTS RESERVED BY PHAIDON PRESS LTD · LONDON SW7
FIRST PUBLISHED 1950
SECOND EDITION 1969

PHAIDON PUBLISHERS INC · NEW YORK
DISTRIBUTORS IN THE UNITED STATES: FREDERICK A. PRAEGER INC
111 FOURTH AVENUE · NEW YORK · N.Y. 10003
LIBRARY OF CONGRESS CATALOG CARD NUMBER: 69–19810

SBN 7148 1388 5
PRINTED AT THE CURWEN PRESS · LONDON E.13
MADE IN GREAT BRITAIN

CONTENTS

FOREWORD

THE plates in this volume illustrate all of the paintings and drawings which I accept as by, or from the workshop of, Uccello. Since these are numerically few, it has been possible to incorporate in the notes a detailed catalogue of the artist's work. Two appendices contain surveys of the lost works of Uccello, and of the paintings and drawings in whose attribution to Uccello I cannot concur. Quotations from Vasari and other early sources are given in English in the Introduction and in Italian throughout the notes. The relatively large number of documents referring to Uccello has been assembled by Boeck (*Paolo Uccello*, 1939, pp. 94–109) and Mather ('Documents mostly new relating to Florentine Painters and Sculptors in the Fifteenth Century' in *The Art Bulletin*, xxx, 1948, pp. 62–4); transcripts of these have been omitted from the present book.

The first debt of all critics is to previous writers in their field, and I must acknowledge a special obligation to the volumes of Salmi and Boeck on Uccello, to Berenson's *Drawings of the Florentine Painters*, and to the articles of Paatz, Pudelko, and Schlosser. I am also personally indebted to Commendatore Giovanni Poggi for facilities for study of the Chiostro Verde frescoes; to Professor Roberto Longhi and Professor Richard Offner for discussion of a number of disputed points; to Mr. John White for elucidating certain problems arising from Uccello's handling of perspective; to Professor Ugo Procacci, to whom is due the discovery of the supplementary frescoes at San Miniato illustrated in this volume, Graf Anton Lanckoronski, Mrs. Shapley, of the National Gallery of Art in Washington, Dr. W. R. Valentiner, Signora Vavalà, and Dr. Johannes Wilde; and to Mr. Ludwig Goldscheider for constant assistance in the preparation of this book.

1949   JOHN POPE-HENNESSY

FOREWORD TO THE SECOND EDITION

WHEN the first edition of this book appeared, it was described by Professor Roberto Longhi as antediluvian. The reason for this was that the catalogue of works presented in it was traditional, and that Uccello's authorship of a number of minor paintings which had been identified as his work was explicitly denied. The bulk of the panel paintings wrongly ascribed to Uccello were exhibited in Florence together in 1954, and neither then nor subsequently have I found any reason materially to modify the views that I expressed. More recently, the transfer of the frescoes ascribed to Uccello in the Duomo at Prato has revealed underdrawings or *sinopie* which are totally at variance with the authentic *sinopie* of Uccello.

The principal additions to our knowledge of Uccello are the outcome of a highly responsible and admirably executed campaign of restoration undertaken by the Soprintendenza alle Gallerie in Florence. The earlier and later frescoes from the Chiostro Verde have been cleaned since 1949, as has the 'Hawkwood' in the Cathedral. The face of the clock painted by Uccello in the Cathedral has been recovered, and the perspective scheme beneath the fresco from San Martino alla Scala has been disclosed. Other paintings cleaned include the 'St. George and the Dragon' and the panel of 'The Rout of San Romano' in the National Gallery in London, and the Urbino predella of 'The Profanation of the Host'. One panel, the 'Portrait of a Youth' at Chambéry, has proved on cleaning to be less closely related to Uccello than it appeared to be twenty years ago. Account is taken of these and other changes in the new edition of the book. In revising the catalogue I have been assisted by Mr. Everett Fahy, without whose help the preparation of the present volume would have been a slower, more laborious task.

1969   JOHN POPE-HENNESSY

INTRODUCTION

FROM THE YEAR 1481, when his name appears in Landino's commentary on the *Divine Comedy*, Uccello has been numbered among the pioneers of Florentine Renaissance painting. Never forgotten and then rediscovered, never neglected and then reassessed, he has remained securely in his niche beside the figures of Donatello, Brunelleschi and Masaccio. The traditional interpretation of Uccello's style is summarized in a letter from Ruskin to Kate Greenaway: 'I believe the perfection of perspective is only recent. It was first applied in Italian art by Paul Uccello. He went off his head with love of perspective.' Time has dealt more severely with Uccello's work than with that of most great artists. Comparatively few paintings survive, and the impression that they leave today is very different from any that they can have made on his contemporaries; the frescoes which were regarded in the sixteenth century as his most signal achievement are abraded or effaced. From these elusive relics the student of Uccello must reconstruct not only the methods by which he represented space, but the part these methods played in the mysterious complex of his personality.

Paolo Uccello was born in 1397. His father, Dono di Paolo, a barber-surgeon from Pratovecchio in the Casentino, had been a citizen of Florence since 1373, and in 1387 had married Uccello's mother, Antonia di Giovanni Castelli del Beccuto. There is no indication of the source from which the painter obtained the name Uccello, but this evidently had some formal sanction, since the only signed works by the artist are inscribed PAVLI VCCELLI or VCIELI OPVS and the name is also used in documents. Vasari tells us that Uccello, like many other artists of his day, was trained in the workshop of the sculptor Ghiberti. We have confirmation of this in a list of the members of Ghiberti's studio made in June 1407, which includes the name of 'Pagolo di Dono, garzone di bottega'. The annual wage paid by Ghiberti to his assistants and apprentices varied from five florins to seventy-five, and Uccello as a new entrant was paid at the lowest rate. Donatello withdrew from the workshop in the year in which Uccello's apprenticeship began, leaving behind him the painter Masolino, a youth of twenty-three, and a boy a year older than Uccello, the architect and sculptor Michelozzo. A few years later, probably in 1412, Uccello's name appears again as the recipient of twenty-five florins a year; and it is likely that he remained a member of the studio until 1414, when, as a painter, he joined the Compagnia di San Luca, or 1415, when 'Paulus olim doni pictor' was admitted to the guild of the Medici e Speciali.

Between 1407 and 1415 the workshop of Ghiberti was the main Florentine stronghold of International Gothic, the sophisticated style which had spread southwards from the courts of Bohemia and Burgundy by way of Milan and Verona to Central Italy. This style, with its pervasive linear rhythms, its reflections of northern metalwork, and the naturalism which found expression in the foliage round Ghiberti's first bronze door, must have made its mark upon Uccello, who would have been present in the studio while the master was evolving the designs for the earlier panels of the first door, and who may well have helped to supervise the casting of the figure of Saint John the Baptist, completed for the guild oratory of Or San Michele in 1414. On many members of the studio Ghiberti's style left no more than a superficial stamp, but with Uccello, as with his older contemporary Masolino, the lessons inculcated in the workshop bore fruit; and in the early fourteen-thirties the shadow of Ghiberti falls across his first surviving works.

Of Uccello's activity during the next ten years, nothing is known. Perhaps he joined forces with some International Gothic painter, Starnina or Lorenzo Monaco; perhaps he remained in the Ghiberti studio. In Florence he would have seen Donatello's St. George and St. Louis of Toulouse installed in their places on Or San Michele, and the St. John the Evangelist set up on the Duomo. He would have listened to discussion of Brunelleschi's project for the cupola of the cathedral, and would have witnessed, in the 'Virgin and Child with St. Anne' painted by Masolino and Masaccio for Sant'Ambrogio, the emergence of the monumental style which after 1424 was worked out on the walls of the Brancacci Chapel. But his experiences of the old art would have outnumbered his experiences of the new, for the style of the future lay hidden in a forest of decorative Gothic paintings, the 'Coronations of the Virgin' of Lorenzo Monaco (1413) and Rossello di Jacopo Franchi (1420), the Bigallo altar-piece of Mariotto di Nardo, Bicci di Lorenzo's frescoes in Santa Lucia (1423), and, last and most important, Gentile da Fabriano's 'Adoration of the Magi' in Santa Trinita (1423) and the Quaratesi polyptych in San Niccolò (1425).

In the year in which the Quaratesi polyptych was set up, Uccello left Florence for Venice, perhaps under an arrangement promoted by Ghiberti, who had been in Venice for three months of the preceding year. A will of 5 August 1425, in which the artist expresses the wish to be buried in his father's tomb in Santo Spirito and names the hospital of Santa Maria Nuova as his legatees, was probably made with this journey in mind. From a document of 1432 we learn that Uccello was employed in Venice as a master mosaicist at St. Mark's. The term 'master mosaicist' connotes a working knowledge of mosaic technique, and if, as is probable, Uccello was appointed to a vacancy advertised by the Venetian Senate in March 1424, he was no doubt trained as a mosaicist in Florence. Uccello was still in Venice in 1427, when a tax return was put in on his behalf, but had returned to Florence by January 1431. Venice was thus the main scene of his activity from 1425 till 1430. The only work he is recorded as executing in these years, a mosaic figure of St. Peter set up in 1425 on the façade of St. Mark's, is lost, but an attempt has been made to trace his hand in the most important of the fifteenth-century mosaics inside the basilica, the 'Scenes from the Life of the Virgin' in the Cappella Mascoli (Figs. XVII–XVIII). Uccello's share in the decoration of the chapel is hypothetical. This early experience of mosaic was to be reflected three decades later in the decorative palette of 'The Rout of San Romano'.

Gentile da Fabriano had come to Florence fresh from triumphs gained in Venice, and in 1425 the great fresco of the naval battle of Salvore, which he had painted in the Sala del Maggior Consiglio of the Ducal Palace, was one of the city's most celebrated sights. The wealth of natural observation compressed into Gentile's 'Adoration of the Magi' (Fig. 1) must have won Uccello's admiration and respect, and the fresco in the Ducal Palace, in which Facio tells us that the artist contrived to represent a hurricane 'with such reality as to strike terror into the spectators', may have inspired his masterpiece, 'The Flood'. Without Gentile's fresco

1. GENTILE DA FABRIANO: THE ADORATION OF THE MAGI. *Uffizi, Florence*

and without the Venetian frescoes of Pisanello, we know too little of Venetian painting in the period during which Uccello was in Venice to establish his indebtedness to individual works of art. But the altar-pieces of Gentile, the early drawings of his pupil Jacopo Bellini (whom Uccello may have known in Florence in 1423), and the sketch-books of Pisanello afford a composite impression of the stylistic influences to which he was subjected in North Italy. In Florence, naturalism, as it was understood during the 1420s by Masaccio and Donatello, was bound up with the rendering of the human form. In North Italy, on the other hand, it involved a far less systematic study of a wider range of physical phenomena. The scope of this can be gauged from the Pisanello sketch-books, with their drawings of plants, grass and trees, horses and greyhounds, birds and butterflies, and from that visual encyclopedia, the fresco of St. George (Fig. 2). This empirical naturalism must have made a decisive impact on Uccello, for feature after feature in the works of his maturity recalls the drawings of the North Italian

3

2. PISANELLO: SAINT GEORGE AND THE DRAGON. *Sant'Anastasia, Verona*

naturalists. Vasari's life contains a reference to 'chests full of drawings' left by the artist, among them studies of 'birds and wonderfully fine animals'. The zoological drawings which passed under Uccello's name in Vasari's *Libro de' Disegni* (Fig. XLII) are by other artists. But examination of Uccello's work suggests that much of his effort must, as Vasari's narrative implies, have gone into the preparation of naturalistic studies, and that his creative procedure may in this respect have been analogous to Pisanello's.

In March 1432 the Florentine orator in Venice was instructed by the Operaii of the Duomo to inquire whether the mosaic figure executed by Uccello for St. Mark's was satisfactory, how his reputation stood and at what rate he had been paid. An autograph tax return prepared in May of the following year shows that by then Uccello was once more resident in Florence. The Florence of 1433 was a very different city from the Florence of 1424. In the Brancacci frescoes and the 'Trinity' Masaccio had invested the human figure with a new dignity, and had evolved new methods of depicting space; and the influence of his personality had penetrated even the conservative precincts of San Marco, where Fra Angelico was completing his 'Madonna dei Linaiuoli'. Within nine short years the vocation of the painter had been transformed; the artificer of the first quarter of the century had become the superman, proficient in the liberal arts, for whose guidance Alberti in 1436 composed his *Della Pittura*. There is nothing in the first work executed after his return to Florence to indicate that Uccello was associated at an early stage with the leaders of this revolution; and when, in 1438, the young Domenico Veneziano, in a letter to Piero de' Medici, enumerates the leading painters working in Florence at that time, he mentions the names of Fra Angelico and Fra Filippo Lippi, but not that of Uccello.

For our knowledge of his early style we are dependent on two undocumented frescoes which all early sources are agreed in regarding as Uccello's. These frescoes, a lunette with 'The Creation of the Animals' and 'The Creation of Adam', and an oblong space beneath with 'The Creation of Eve' and 'The Fall' (Pls. 1–10), are described by Vasari: 'He was afterwards allotted some scenes in the cloister of Santa Maria Novella. The first of these is where one enters the church from the cloister, and represents the creation of the animals, with an infinite number of different creatures, fishes, beasts, and birds. Since he was very fanciful and, as I have said, took great delight in making animals well, he showed the pride of some lions, eager to fight, and the fleetness and timidity of certain stags and bucks, in addition to which the birds and fishes with their feathers and scales are very lively. Here also he made the creation of man and of woman, with their sin, in a beautiful style, carefully and finely executed. In this work he took pleasure in the colouring of the trees, which had not usually been well done up to that time. Thus he was the first among the old painters to earn a reputation for portraying landscapes.' Situated at the north end of the east wall of the cloister, the two frescoes form part of a cycle of scenes from the Old Testament, of which those on the south and west walls had been completed not long before by two pedestrian Gothic artists. The earlier scenes are executed largely in *terra verde* (green earth), whence the cloister obtained its name of Chiostro Verde. Relieved by a dull red background and by local colour in the yellow perspective haloes, the yellow edging of the robes, and the blue and red flowers sprinkled across the grass, this pigment determines the tonality of Uccello's scenes. The two frescoes are separated by a parti-coloured string-course drawn in perspective. Linear perspective as such, however, plays no part in either scene, and the landscape of the lunette with its conventionalized rocks recalls the landscape backgrounds employed by another Florentine Gothic artist, Masolino, in the almost contemporary frescoes at Castiglione d'Olona. The lunette is dominated by two likenesses of God the Father, one in left profile, impassive and statuesque, its half-Gothic, half-classical drapery reminiscent of the 'St. Matthew' of Ghiberti (Fig. 3): the other in right profile, moving forwards, the action of the legs visible beneath the drapery and the right arm outstretched. A model by Ghiberti must also have been in the painter's mind (and may actually have been before his eyes) when he prepared the cartoon for the seated Adam, which is based in reverse on a figure in a classical sarcophagus that also inspired the Adam in Ghiberti's second bronze door (Fig. 4). To the left, like the aggregated contents of some Lombard naturalist's sketch-book, appear the animals, some, such as the stag and ass, conceived in realistic terms, others the product of the literal imagination which is reported by Vasari to have led the artist who had 'never seen a chameleon . . . to represent it as a large and awkward camel swallowing air'. The lions described by Vasari appear only in the under-drawing (*sinopia*) beneath the fresco (Pl. 1). The lower scene is seriously damaged and without the *sinopia* could not be fully understood. On the left the figure of Adam has disappeared, and of the Eve only the upper part survives, but the under-drawing reveals that in the noble God the Father in benediction and the sleeping Adam Uccello again drew his inspiration from Ghiberti. Unlike the lunette, the lower fresco is deployed without recession across a single plane. Whereas the trees in the upper scene diminish naturalistically, the foliage in the scene

5

3. GHIBERTI: SAINT MATTHEW. *Or San Michele, Florence*

below is treated like a tapestry. From one tree there hang the orange fruit which are a recurrent decorative feature of Uccello's work. On the right of the scene Adam and Eve are ranged beside the tree, the Adam related to the Eve in the 'Temptation' of Ghiberti and the Eve related to the corresponding figure in Ghiberti's 'Expulsion from Paradise'. The head of Eve is more clearly discernible in the *sinopia* than in the fresco. On the other hand, the exquisitely delicate profile of the serpent is developed in the fresco to a point which far transcends the summary indications in the *sinopia*, and the hair in particular, much of which survives intact, is delineated with the delicacy of a sketch by Pisanello. Throughout the frescoes the monumental forms and the sustained seriousness of the narrative intention reveal an artist of uncommon force; and something of the spirit of Pico della Mirandola's *De Hominis Dignitate* is captured in the scene in which God, the 'divine architect', sets Adam in the centre of 'this terrestrial dwelling, this august temple of divinity which is our world'. In terms of style the two frescoes introduce us to two characteristics of Uccello's art. The first is a predilection for the virtual monochrome of *terra verde* as a medium for external or architecturally sited frescoes (no fewer than six of Uccello's surviving frescoes and two lost fresco cycles were carried out in this technique), and the second is its corollary, a relief-like style whose affinities are with sculpture not with painting.

4. GHIBERTI: THE CREATION
OF ADAM AND EVE AND THE
EXPULSION FROM PARADISE
(from the *Porta del Paradiso*).
Baptistry, Florence

The task for which Uccello was destined by the Duomo authorities in 1432 seems to have involved some form of mosaic decoration, but there is no evidence that he was actually employed in the Cathedral before 1436, when he engaged to paint a monumental effigy of Sir John Hawkwood (Pls. 12–15). Hawkwood, the London tailor's apprentice who raised himself to knighthood under Edward III and ended his career in Florence as a successful leader of mercenary troops, had died in 1394. A year before his death provision was made for a marble monument to be erected above his grave in the Cathedral, but this expensive project was not proceeded with, and at the end of 1395 a commemorative fresco was commissioned from Agnolo Gaddi, the last survivor of one of the great painter families of the trecento. Taste, however, changed, and by 1433 it was decided that the fresco of Gaddi, stiff and antiquated as it must have been, should be replaced. For three years action was deferred, but in 1436 it was agreed that a new memorial should be substituted. On 30 May Uccello was ordered to replace Gaddi's fresco with a fresco in *terra verde*, on 28 June he was instructed to efface the horse and rider he had executed on the wall 'because it was not painted as it should be', on 6 July he was told to make a new attempt, and by the end of August the fresco was complete. The erasure of the first version was probably due to some technical defect in the preparation of the ground, and not, as is often implied, to dissatisfaction with Uccello's cartoon.

The 'Hawkwood' shows the mounted figure of the condottiere in profile to the right on a sarcophagus supported by three consoles projecting from the wall. In the first half of the fifteenth century the equestrian sepulchral monument, though uncommon, was not unknown

7

5. MONUMENT OF PAOLO SAVELLI (d. 1405).
Santa Maria dei Frari, Venice

in Tuscany. It has been suggested that a North Italian wooden tomb, of the class of the pig-mented Savelli monument in the church of the Frari at Venice (Fig. 5), was in Uccello's mind. But as early as 1390 a wooden equestrian figure of this type was to be seen in Florence above a doorway in the Campanile. The horse depicted by Uccello, on the other hand, depends directly from a prototype in Venice, the classical bronze horses of St. Mark's, which were much studied by North Italian artists and a sketch of which appears concurrently in a North Italian drawing at Bergamo (Fig. 6). Two decades later, when he came to represent another mounted condottiere, Micheletto Attendoli da Cotignola in the Louvre 'Rout of San Romano', Uccello again based the riding figure on the antique. The work of Ghiberti offers many precedents for this practice of direct quotation from classical originals. In the sixteenth century the horse of the 'Hawkwood' was criticized by Vasari as being 'represented as moving his legs on one side only, a thing horses cannot do without falling'; this criticism, often repeated in later times, is based on a misunderstanding of the pose selected by Uccello. Both horse and rider are shown without foreshortening. A squared preliminary drawing for the upper part of the monument, now in the Uffizi (Pl. 11), in some respects affords

6. NORTH ITALIAN: STUDY AFTER THE HORSES OF SAINT MARK'S. *Accademia Carrara, Bergamo*

7. MASACCIO: MADONNA AND CHILD.
National Gallery, London

a clearer indication of the artist's original intention than the fresco as it exists today. In this sheet the hindquarters of the horse are represented as a circle and the neck as an arc. The attempt to rationalize natural forms by assimilating them to a geometrical equivalent recurs in 'The Rout of San Romano' and the later frescoes in the Chiostro Verde.

Since the fresco was intended as a substitute for a monument in three dimensions, it was incumbent on the artist to establish an illusion of tridimensionality. This is now impaired by a flat decorative border added in the early sixteenth century. If tradition is to be believed, the technique of perspective representation was first worked out by Brunelleschi, the architect, and in painting its function was conceived initially as that of reproducing architectural forms. It is employed in this way in the Pisa polyptych of Masaccio (1426), where the Virgin, now in the National Gallery, is seated on a Brunelleschan throne (Fig. 7), and in the Brunelleschan architecture of Masaccio's 'Trinity'. The architecture of the 'Hawkwood', with its sharp recession and low vanishing point, makes use of the same technical procedure as these works. What is peculiar to Uccello is a preoccupation (apparent in the pattern of receding studs above the coats of arms and in the ribbon that runs along the lid of the sarcophagus) with the ornamental possibilities of the technique.

In 1443, seven years after the painting of the 'Hawkwood', we find Uccello once more at work in the Cathedral, engaged on a commission, the painting of the clock-face at the west end

9

The Clock-Face and the Windows in the Duomo

8. GHIBERTI: HEAD OF VITTORIO GHIBERTI
(from the *Porta del Paradiso*). *Baptistry, Florence*

of the church, which involved the use of linear perspective to create an illusory architectural scheme. This scheme (Fig. 111) is founded on the formula of a circle inscribed within a square, which recurs on the base of the 'Hawkwood'. Both square and circle are depicted in recession framing the dial of the clock, the interior of which is coloured blue and had at its centre a gold star. In the spandrels are circular apertures, containing the most striking pictorial feature of the work, four large male heads (Pls. 25–8). It is possible that the motif of a male head thrust through an *œil-de-bœuf* was suggested to Uccello by the Porta del Paradiso of Ghiberti (Fig. 8), but in style the colossal heads, with their bold planes and realistic detail, belong rather to the world of Donatello's 'Habakkuk'. Uccello's differs from the rather similar scheme shown in the *De Prospettiva Pingendi* of Piero della Francesca (Fig. 9), in that the heads are represented without foreshortening.

To the summer and autumn of 1443 belong three cartoons for the circular windows in the cupola of Santa Maria del Fiore, representing 'The Ascension', 'The Resurrection', and 'The Nativity'. These were followed early in 1444 by a fourth cartoon of 'The Annunciation'. In the case of 'The Ascension' Uccello's cartoon was rejected in favour of a cartoon of the same subject by Ghiberti, but the three remaining designs were executed in stained glass. Two of these windows survive. It was the normal practice for the drawing on the glass to be undertaken by the glass-painter, not by the artist responsible for the cartoon; and Uccello's 'Nativity' and 'Resurrection' (Pls. 29, 30) are for this reason coarsely executed. In 'The Resurrection' this affects not only the receding perspective of the tomb (a feature which links the composition to the frescoes at San Miniato), but the figures of the sleeping soldiers on each side; and the most successful figure is that of the risen Christ, which retains the Gothic rhythm of the Eve in the Chiostro Verde and is seen against a wheel of light. The 'Nativity', dominated by the rectangular structure of the stable, is also Ghibertesque. Since Ghiberti was the principal

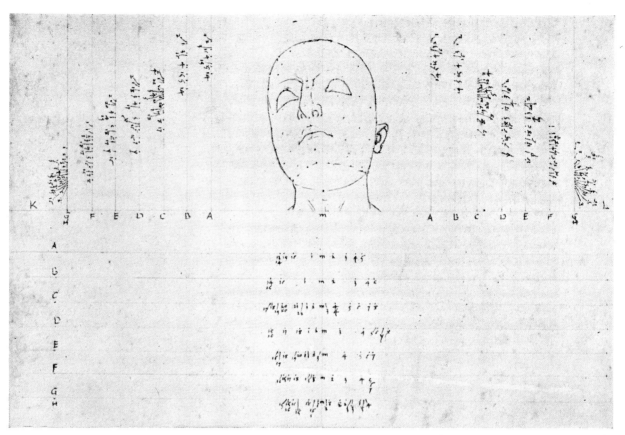

9. PIERO DELLA FRANCESCA: STUDY OF A FORESHORTENED HEAD FROM THE 'DE PROSPETTIVA PINGENDI'

designer of stained glass for the Cathedral and himself contributed some of the finest of the cartoons for the windows in the cupola, it is not unnatural that Uccello's windows should continue to reflect Ghiberti's personality at a time when his pictorial style was already liberated from Ghiberti's influence.

The commissions for the Cathedral were followed, probably at a few years' remove, by another work mentioned by Vasari, the 'Scenes from Monastic Legends' on the east wall of the cloister at San Miniato al Monte (Pls. 17–24; Figs. 1–11). These frescoes, originally eight in number, belong to a class of cloister decoration of which earlier examples are a fresco of 'The Reform of the Carmelite Order' in the cloister of the Carmine (1432) and the 'Scenes from the Life of St. Benedict' in the Chiostro degli Aranci of the Badia (late thirties). A cognate cycle of 'Scenes from the Life of St. Benedict', now lost, was executed by Uccello (probably in the mid-thirties) in *terra verde* in the Chiostro degli Angeli. The colouristic effect of the San Miniato frescoes is described in Vasari's *Life*: 'In San Miniato, outside Florence, he did the cloister partly in *verde terra* and partly in colour, representing the lives of the Holy Fathers, in which he did not carefully observe a proper consistency in the employment of his colours, for he made his fields blue, his city red, and his buildings of various hues according to his fancy. In this he was at fault, for buildings which are represented to be of stone cannot and ought not to be coloured another tint.' Vasari's account is confirmed by the frescoes in their present sadly damaged state. With their *terra verde* figures and yellow perspective haloes, pink and red buildings and green grass, their tonality cannot have been far removed from that

The Costruzione Legittima

of the pink and green Santa Lucia altar-piece of Domenico Veneziano (late forties). The aesthetic interest of the frescoes resides, however, less in their colour than in their construction, for they are the first works of Uccello in which the system of linear perspective employed for the string-course in the Chiostro Verde and for the architecture of the 'Hawkwood' extends into the picture space. Throughout the greater part of the cycle the frescoed area has been reduced to a narrow strip, but two scenes, those at the north and south ends of the east wall, retain their full size. In the first the receding lines of a wall on the left and of a flight of steps on the right, and in the second the upper and lower edges of a building on the left and a furrow in the ground, meet in a vanishing point set in the centre of the fresco at a uniform height from the base. So far as can be judged, this formula was common to all of the scenes on the east wall.

To understand this scheme we must turn aside for a moment to consider the system on which it is based, the perspective procedure known as *costruzione legittima* which had been developed early in the century by Brunelleschi and which is described in the *Della Pittura* of Alberti. The *costruzione legittima* (Fig. 10) was a method of depicting space. At its simplest (and the procedure was susceptible of many variations) the base of the picture space was divided into an arbitrary number of equal sections, which were joined with the vanishing point. The resulting lines supplied the orthogonals of the composition. The exact location of the vanishing point might be further to the right or left (at San Miniato, as we have seen, it falls in the exact centre of the fresco field), but ideally its height was predetermined by the height of a human figure standing, or imagined as standing, in the front plane of the painting. A further calculation gave the artist the optimum distance of the eye from the projection plane, and this was expressed by means of a line (on the same horizontal as the vanishing point) drawn from a vertical erected at a corner of the base to a point outside the picture space. The latter point was then connected with the bases of the orthogonals. Each of the new lines necessarily cut the vertical, and horizontal lines drawn through these points of intersection demarcated the receding planes of the design.

The purpose of the *costruzione legittima* was to facilitate pictorial realism; it was, that is to say, a means of equating the imaginary world within the painting with the real world in front

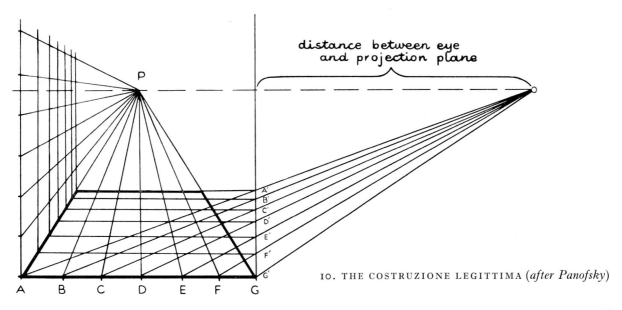

10. THE COSTRUZIONE LEGITTIMA (*after Panofsky*)

11. DOMENICO VENEZIANO: A MIRACLE OF SAINT ZENOBIUS. *Fitzwilliam Museum, Cambridge*

of the spectator's eyes. But the 'legitimate construction' did not proceed from the thing seen, was indeed an abstract intellectual discipline, which the painter, according to his temperament, might use in a more or a less realistic way. In the predella of the Santa Lucia altar-piece of Domenico Veneziano (Fig. 11), for example, it is employed as a means of ensuring pictorial veracity, and not as an aesthetic device in its own right. But in the hands of Uccello at San Miniato its function is first and foremost to establish a visual pattern throughout the entire wall, and the artist's concern is with its formal rather than its realistic possibilities. Where Domenico Veneziano creates a space illusion to lend body to his figures and substance to his narrative, Uccello deals in space for its own sake. The figures at San Miniato, almost invariably placed in the front plane of the fresco, are isolated in a vacuum of space, and the construction behind them remains void and theoretical. Details like the portrayal of the surfaces of a machicolated wall in one of the two central scenes form a self-imposed exercise in pictorial virtuosity. Within the figures (as in the preliminary drawing for the 'Hawkwood') the forms are geometricized. This predisposition towards pattern is apparent in the round head of a

The Flood

tonsured friar (Pl. 20), and in the exquisite profile of a fair-haired angel set on its halo like a medallic portrait (Pl. 24).

Few of the documentary references to Uccello in these years relate to extant works. From tax returns put in in 1446 and 1458 we learn that he was living in a house in the Via della Scala, near the church of Santa Lucia d'Ognissanti, and that he rented a workshop in the Piazza San Giovanni. In 1453 his wife, Tommasa di Benedetto Malifici, gave birth to a son, Donato, and three years later to a daughter, Antonia. In 1450 he received a payment for the painting of a tabernacle in San Giovanni; further payments were made, through the Cambini bank, for an unspecified painting in December 1451 and February 1452; in 1453 he painted a figure of the Beato Andrea Corsini for the Library of the Cathedral; in 1455 he was working for San Miniato al Monte; and in 1456 he was associated in the preparation of cartoons for two windows with the glass-painter, Bernardo di Francesco, who had been responsible for carrying out the window of 'The Resurrection' in the Duomo. This long period of residence in Florence was interrupted by a visit to Padua, which is recorded by Vasari in the words: 'Paolo was taken by Donato to Padua when the latter was working there'. No doubt it was in the course of this visit that Uccello painted the 'giants in chiaroscuro' in the Casa dei Vitaliani near the Eremitani, which Mantegna is reported to have admired. Donatello was employed in Padua from 1443 to 1453 on the bronze Crucifix for the Santo, the high altar of the church and the statue of Gattamelata, and Uccello's visit may have occurred at any time during these years. Intimacy with Donatello would have brought him into contact not only with the greatest sculptor of the fifteenth century, but also with the artist who had made the most extensive and most individual contribution to the technique of portraying space. At about the time Uccello was employed on the earlier Chiostro Verde frescoes, Donatello was devising the elaborate recession of the 'Ascension with Christ giving the Keys to St. Peter' in London; while Uccello was at work on the 'Hawkwood', Donatello was evolving the complex linear patterns of the stucco roundels in the Sagrestia Vecchia of San Lorenzo. The 'Ascension', and still more the roundels, argue a practical mastery of perspective incomparably greater than Uccello's at that time; and if the visit to Padua took place in or about 1447, when Donatello's relief of 'The Miracle of the Penitent Son' (Fig. 12) was already an accomplished fact, it might well be that the influence of this and cognate designs by Donatello was responsible for the decisive advance evident in his next Florentine commission, the fresco of 'The Flood' (Pls. 31, 33–42).

Like the earlier scenes in the Chiostro Verde, the fresco of 'The Flood' is so severely damaged that many of the incidents contained in it are no longer clear. Some of them are elucidated by a description prepared by Vasari at a time when the fresco was more fully visible than it is today: 'When he had completed this task, he worked in the same cloister beneath two scenes by the hands of other artists, painting the Flood and Noah's ark, representing the dead, the tempest, the fury of the winds, the flashes of lightning, the rooting up of trees, and the terror of men, with such pains and with so much art and diligence, that no more can be said. In perspective he has represented a dead body, foreshortened, the eyes of which are being pecked out by a crow, and a drowned child, whose body, being full of water, is arched up. He further represented various human emotions, such as the disregard of the water by two fighting men on horseback, the extreme terror of death of a woman and a man who are riding astride a buffalo; but as his hind parts are sinking they are despairing of all hope of safety. The work is of such quality and excellence that Paolo acquired the greatest fame from it. His diminution of the figures, by means of perspective, and his representation of

14

12. DONATELLO: THE MIRACLE OF THE PENITENT SON. *Sant'Antonio, Padua*

mazzocchi and other things, is certainly very beautiful.' The *mazzocchi* to which Vasari refers were male headdresses of wood or wicker, which supported the *foggia* and *becchetto*; by virtue of their form, they presented a representational problem of great structural complexity. Other details are explained by an outline engraving (Fig. IV) made, when the fresco was already much abraded, for the *Storia della pittura italiana* of Rosini (1839).

In common with the frescoes which precede it, the lunette represents two separate scenes, on the left 'The Flood' and on the right 'The Recession of the Flood'. The first shows the corner and side of the ark. In the left foreground is a naked man on horseback brandishing a sword, perhaps, as Vasari supposed, engaged in combat with a nude youth in left profile, with a *mazzocchio* round his neck, holding a club. Between the two floats the almost obliterated body of a drowning boy. Behind, a figure in full length clings in desperation to the narrow ledge that runs along the ark. In the centre foreground is a woman seen from behind seated on an ox or cow, the sole survivor of the 'woman and man who are riding on a buffalo' noted by Vasari, and to her right is a fully clad male figure, whose ankles are grasped by a drowning man. Further back are a naked youth floating in a barrel, two swimming figures, one of them supporting himself on an upturned cask, a naked man on a raft, accompanied by a bear and using a club to ward off some swimming animal, and a man scrambling on to the edge of the ark. In the distance a number of smaller figures, among them two women crouching on the ground, are only partly decipherable. On the right we look across the end of the ark. In the foreground are two drowned bodies washed up by the tide, one shown feet foremost, the other with its head towards the spectator; between them is the 'dead body . . . whose eyes are being pecked out by a crow'; and further back is another detail mentioned by Vasari, the 'drowned child whose body, being full of water, is arched up'. Above, at the window of the ark, appears the figure of the patriarch Noah, stretching out his hand to the returning dove. The combination of *terra verde*, indian red, brown, yellow, and (in the case of the distant tree, branches of which are blown by the tornado towards the foreground of the fresco) green is the same as in the earlier scenes.

The fact that in this lunette alone the two scenes depicted are grouped under a common title, 'The Flood', is a commentary on Uccello's composition, since the two representations

The Construction of The Flood

of the ark converge, and what in point of time are two dissociated episodes are thus united in a single visual scheme. The procedure which underlies 'The Flood' is essentially the same as at San Miniato, but its application is more elaborate and more logical. It is more elaborate in that the standing male figure in the right foreground determines the height of the vanishing point above the base of the fresco; that one of the orthogonals survives in the edge of a ladder lying on the ground on the left side of the scene; and that the diminishing perspective of the rungs of the ladder and the planks of the ark serves to indicate the multiplicity of transverse lines by means of which the space recession must have been worked out. It is more logical in that figures are distributed through the entire picture space, and the pyramidal design is thus justified as a narrative, and not merely as a decorative, expedient.

The *Della Pittura* explains more of 'The Flood' than its constructional technique. Here is objectified Alberti's ideal of the copious composition, 'in which, in their appropriate places, are combined old men and young, youths, women, girls, and children, fowls and small birds, horses and sheep, buildings, provinces and all similar things', portrayed in all their natural variety, but with moderation, dignity, and truth. Here are the variations of costume and pose advocated by Alberti, some figures clothed, some naked, some seated, some kneeling, some lying down. Here are 'motions of the spirit' expressed, as Alberti demands, through the movements of the body and the face. Here are the living bodies, 'alive in all the smallest parts', juxtaposed with dead. Here (in the foremost figure clinging to the ark) is the wind-swept drapery, here (in the youth with the *mazzocchio*) the wind-swept hair which it delighted Alberti to observe, and here (in the right background) is the embodiment of the south or west wind 'which breathes through the clouds from the point from which the draperies are blown'. In 'The Flood' these dry, rather scholastic concepts are quickened by a vital pictorial vision, a forceful imagination which relives, in all its horror, the cataclysm that overwhelms mankind.

In the rectangle below 'The Flood' are the two scenes of 'Noah's Sacrifice' and 'The Drunkenness of Noah' (Pls. 32, 43–48). The lower parts of both are lost, and we are dependent for an understanding of the first on an engraving reproduced by Seroux d'Agincourt (1823) (Fig. v), and of the second on an engraving by Calendi (1791) (Fig. vi). No attempt is made to combine the two scenes, though the vine-covered trellis which divides them converges on a vanishing point falling directly beneath that in the lunette above. The scene on the left is described by Vasari in these terms: 'He further made the sacrifice of Noah, the ark being open in perspective, with ranges of perches in the upper parts divided into regular rows where the birds are stationed, which fly out in flocks foreshortened in several directions. In the air appears God the Father above the sacrifice which Noah and his sons are making. This is the most difficult figure represented by Paolo in all his works, because it is flying towards the wall with the head foreshortened, and it has such force, and is in such strong relief, that it has the appearance of forcing its way through. Besides this, Noah is surrounded by a large number of different animals of great excellence.' The perches, birds, and animals have vanished, but the foreshortened altar, the eight kneeling figures and the inverted God the Father beneath a rainbow survive, damaged and almost colourless, to bear their pallid tribute to the amplitude of the artist's forms. Though we are the poorer for the loss of the details that impressed themselves upon Vasari, we may find compensation in the eloquent gesture of the patriarch as he performs his act of invocation, and in the shrouded figure of his wife.

In 'The Drunkenness of Noah', the body of Noah, a wine cask described by Vasari ('made in perspective, the curved lines being considered very fine'), and all but the faintest traces of a

16

second cask depicted end foremost on the right, have disappeared, but the dark-blue ground visible through the trellis, the green leaves and purple grapes, and the yellow and brown of the plaited straw hut on the right afford some indication of the original colouring of the scene. A *sinopia* disclosed in 1909, when the fresco was taken from the wall, reveals as an afterthought one of the most distinctive features of this part of the painting, the circular head of Shem gazing out of the fresco in full face. In conformity with the narrative in Genesis, Shem is shown walking backwards, while Japhet averts his eyes from his father's nakedness. The head of Ham, who appears in profile outside the hut pointing towards Noah's body, seems to be a portrait, and was supposed in the time of Vasari to represent the painter Dello Delli. Whether or not this tradition is correct, the treatment of the profile recalls that in the only portrait drawing ascribed to Uccello, a study of a male head in the Uffizi (Pl. 50), which must have been made at about the same time as the frescoes.

The perspective of 'The Flood' and 'The Drunkenness of Noah' recurs in a yet more evolved form in a somewhat later work, a fresco of 'The Nativity' formerly in the cloister of San Martino alla Scala (Pls. 83–4). Like the frescoes in the Chiostro Verde, 'The Nativity' is executed in *terra verde* with some local colouring, brown for the supports framing the stable, reddish-brown for the interior of the stable roof, yellow or yellowish-white for the sheep on the left, and green for the distant trees. Even more damaged than the earlier scenes, the fresco from San Martino preserves its incised orthogonals and transversals (Fig. xv), and it is likely that these were always intended to be seen. It is from lost works by Uccello of this class that the patterned backgrounds found in the predella panels of the Sienese Giovanni di Paolo after about 1455 derive. The centre of this fresco is so gravely damaged that it was long assumed to have been planned as two 'legitimate constructions' juxtaposed, with vanishing points on the outer edges of the scene. But when the fresco was taken off the wall and the *sinopia* was revealed, it proved to be an orthodox 'legitimate construction', with a vanishing point in the centre of the lunette and with distance points in the margin to right and left. In Masolino's frescoes in S. Clemente in Rome the architecture in adjacent scenes sometimes diverges from the point of juncture of the frescoes, and it is the same bifocal method, in a more advanced, more rational form, that is used here. Logical as it is, this expedient must always have been disconcerting. Whereas in 'The Flood' Uccello links two separate episodes in a unitary visual scheme, in 'The Nativity' he divides a single scene into two visually discrete parts. Hints are scattered throughout Vasari's biography of the disfavour with which contemporaries regarded Uccello's later work, and we need look no further than the ark-like stable in the San Martino fresco to understand why this was so. Though the technique of space representation employed by Uccello in 'The Nativity' is specifically Florentine, the use to which he puts it is reminiscent of North Italy, and especially of the drawings of Jacopo Bellini, from one of which the small figure of a man suspended from a gallows in the left background of the fresco perhaps derives. Another drawing by Jacopo Bellini (Fig. 13) contains a suggestive parallel for the stable in Uccello's fresco. While naturalistic details redeem, they cannot altogether neutralize the scheme of 'The Nativity'; and our verdict on the class of paintings by Uccello of which this alone survives might well be in the words which Gibbon used of Plato, that 'his poetical imagination sometimes fixed and animated these metaphysical abstractions'.

The impulse towards a decorative, non-illusionistic system of perspective is still more pronounced in the works by which the artist is most generally remembered, the three panels of

13. JACOPO BELLINI: THE NATIVITY. *Louvre, Paris*

'The Rout of San Romano' (Pls. 51–76), now distributed between the National Gallery, the Uffizi, and the Louvre. The battle commemorated in 'The Rout of San Romano' took place on 1 June 1432. Since the preceding April, Florentine territory had been ravaged by Sienese forces under the condottiere Bernardino della Carda, then in alliance with the Duke of Milan. Following a succession of reverses it was decided by the Signoria that Niccolò Maurucci da Tolentino, one of the best known condottieri of the day, should replace the then commander of the Florentine troops, Micheletto Attendoli da Cotignola, who was relegated to the command of a subsidiary force. The new appointment rapidly justified itself, and Niccolò da Tolentino, an impetuous man, pursued the Sienese with such temerity that he lost contact with his main force, and, accompanied by not more than twenty horsemen, was surprised by the Sienese troops under Bernardino della Carda in the Arno valley near the Tower of San Romano. Instead of capitulating, as the military code of the time would have allowed, Niccolò da Tolentino and his small force resisted the Sienese attack and, after fighting for eight hours against heavy odds, were relieved by Micheletto da Cotignola, whose troops, crossing the Arno, set upon the Sienese rear and snatched victory from defeat. 'Three panels of the Rout of San Romano' make their first appearance in an inventory of 1492 of the contents of the Palazzo Medici, when they formed part of the furnishings of the bedroom of Lorenzo de' Medici; they were presumably commissioned by Cosimo de' Medici as part of a scheme of interior decoration which included the painting of the chapel of the palace by Benozzo Gozzoli in 1459 and that of the Sala Grande by Antonio Pollajuolo a year later. It is possible that the commission

14. CASTAGNO: NICCOLÒ DA TOLENTINO.
Duomo, Florence

dates from 1456, when Castagno executed an equestrian figure of Niccolò da Tolentino (Fig. 14) for a position adjacent to Uccello's 'Hawkwood' in the Cathedral.

The inventory of 1492 tells us something not only of the place of origin but of the siting of the panels, which were set in gilded frames or between gilt pilasters above a cupboard, with their lower edges some seven feet or more from the ground. It has, moreover, been revealed by cleaning that the panels were not rectangular, and that the upper corners corresponded with the corbels of the room. Their height may have been greater than it is now, since two of them are cut along the top. The three panels, though they form a decorative whole, were not planned as a continuous narrative, and represent three separate incidents, on the left 'Niccolò da Tolentino directing the Battle of San Romano' (National Gallery), in the centre 'The Unhorsing of Bernardino della Carda' (Uffizi), signed on a cartellino in the lower left corner PAVLI. VCIELI. OPVS, and on the right 'Micheletto da Cotignola attacking the Sienese rear' (Louvre). Throughout, the employment of linear perspective is more limited than in the frescoes which precede them, and is confined to a relatively narrow frontal strip on which the main scene is deployed. The background has no spatial reference to the episode in front, and the compositions resemble scenes played before a drop curtain, in which we are perpetually conscious of a disparity between the false space represented on the backcloth and the real space of the stage. Where linear perspective is used, the treatment recalls that of 'The Flood', and both in the National Gallery and in the Uffizi panels the splintered fragments of lances are arranged on the ground in such a way that, like the

19

ladder and other properties in the fresco, they indicate the orthogonals and transversals of the perspective scheme. Such unity of composition as is imposed on the three panels is achieved by equipoise of forms and colour and not by linear perspective; thus the figure of Niccolò da Tolentino turned to the right on a white horse, beneath a banner with the device of Solomon's knot, in the National Gallery panel is balanced in the panel in the Louvre by the figure of Micheletto da Cotignola, turned to the left on a dark horse, beneath a banner bearing a unicorn, while the central panel is built round a pyramid formed by the white steed of Bernardino della Carda and two horses on the ground, flanked on each side by a white and a grey horse.

Like the horse of the 'Hawkwood', the horses in 'The Rout of San Romano' are constructed round a framework of geometry. This is more evident in the panel in the National Gallery than in the better preserved panels in the Uffizi and the Louvre. Especially in the scene in London it is tempting to dismiss the horses as formalized, but to do this is to misread their character. On the contrary, the horses of 'The Rout' (and there are upwards of two dozen distributed over the three panels) offer a realistic solution of a problem hardly less arduous than that presented by 'The Flood'. Just as 'The Flood', under the inspiration of Alberti, explores an unprecedented range of human gestures and emotions, so 'The Rout of San Romano', possibly in conjunction with Alberti's treatise on the horse, depicts the full repertoire of postures of what, after the human figure, was the canonical subject of Renaissance artists. On the right of the panel in the Louvre, where five heads of horses are shown side by side, the artist's concern with expression is as pronounced as in the earlier painting. Where the 'Hawkwood' looks forward to Donatello's 'Gattamelata', the prancing horses of 'The Rout' anticipate Leonardo's Trivulzio monument; and it is interesting that one of them, the kicking

15. PISANELLO: STUDIES OF THE HEAD OF A HORSE. *Louvre, Paris.* (Vallardi 2354, f. 143)

horse of the Uffizi panel, reappears among the drawings made by Leonardo in connexion with this commission. For the heads of the horses in particular, parallels are to be found in the drawings of Pisanello (Fig. 15), and work on the panels must have been preceded by a long series of naturalistic studies, progenitors of the 'estampe en couleurs, d'un élève de Paolo Uccello, à l'usage des vétérinaires' of *Les Faux-Monnayeurs*.

A high degree of naturalism is also aimed at in the mounted figures, especially in the three knights in combat on the right of the panel in the National Gallery, the falling figure of Bernardino della Carda, and the charging knight on a white horse on the left of the central scene. A drawing in the Uffizi (Pl. 16) has been connected with the latter figure; though this splendid sheet is not a study for 'The Rout of San Romano', the same analysis of movement must have preceded the artist's rendering of the mounted knights. In the panels, however, movement is depicted less effectively than in this preliminary sketch, for repeatedly the painter's realistic impulse is arrested by his interest in details of equipment or costume. The damask cloak and head-dress of Niccolò da Tolentino (who is shown in ceremonial dress and not in the accoutrements he would have worn in battle) might form the background of a Madonna by Giambono; the crossbows held by the foot-soldiers and the poly-chrome *mazzocchi* are treated as objects of beauty in themselves; and the black, red, and yellow lances appear to have no other function than that of establishing fantastic linear patterns against the dark-green trees. Again and again the artist's will to realism is mitigated by his all-pervading decorative sense. The menacing horsemen, faces invisible beneath their helmets, necks shielded by circular rondels, shoulders protected by curved pauldrons, forearms encased in vambraces, knees sheathed in floriated genouillères, are crowned with orchidaceous plumes; and the colour (the silver armour, of which traces remain in the panel in the Louvre, the pale-blue trappings of the horse in the centre of the National Gallery painting, the red and purple shields in the panel on the right) lends the three scenes a veneer of heraldry. But beneath this decorative crust there lies a 'morbidly naturalistic art', which enabled Ruskin to interpret the 'tender red flowers tossing above the helmets and glowing beneath the lowered lances' in 'The Rout of San Romano' as a symbol of 'neglect of the perfectness of the Earth's beauty by reason of the passions of men'.

The three panels of 'The Rout of San Romano' were preceded or followed by four similar scenes, painted for the Casa Bartolini in Valfonda and containing, according to Vasari, 'horses and armed men in the apparel of the time. Among the men are portraits of Paolo Orsino, Ottobuono da Parma, Luca da Canale, and Carlo Malatesta, lord of Rimini, all commanders of that time. These pictures being damaged, and having suffered a good deal, were restored in our own day by Giuliano Bugiardini, who has done them more harm than good.' None of the Bartolini panels survives, and in their place we may pass to two other paintings associable with 'The Rout of San Romano'. The first of these is a panel of 'St. George and the Dragon' in the Musée Jacquemart-André (Pls. 77, 79). The patterned landscape background of this panel connects it with the Uffizi 'Unhorsing of Bernardino della Carda', and the prancing horse seems also to derive from the horses of 'The Rout'. Vasari tells us that the artist painted 'a number of small pictures in perspective for the sides of couches, beds and other things', and it is with these panels that the scene in the Musée Jacquemart-André belongs. The second painting, in the National Gallery in London, is a work of higher calibre (Pls. 78, 80–82). Painted on canvas (like the lost 'Combat of Dragons and Lions' and the 'Serpent struggling with a Lion', which filled part of one of the side walls of the room in the Palazzo Medici

The Profanation of the Host

containing 'The Rout of San Romano'), the London 'St. George and the Dragon' shows the Saint, again on a white horse, plunging diagonally across the picture space with the point of his long lance embedded in the dragon's eye; only the Princess remains in profile, an attenuated and still Gothic figure that might spring from the pages of the *Très Riches Heures*. The barren foreground, broken up by rectangles of grass, recalls that of the battle-picture in the Louvre, while in the background the receding space and distant wood are handled with a sureness and competence for which we look in vain in the Jacquemart-André panel. Above the horizontal lines of cloud that cross the sky there rides a crescent moon which shines down on two other late works by the artist, the Oxford 'Hunt' and the predella of 'The Profanation of the Host' in the Palazzo Ducale at Urbino.

The veil which shrouds Uccello's later life is lifted in 1465, when he appears at Urbino with his son, Donato, to negotiate a contract with the Confraternity of Corpus Domini. There are repeated references to his activity in 1467 and 1468, when he returned to Florence leaving behind him in Urbino a single work, 'The Profanation of the Host' (Pls. 87–100). It is presumed, almost certainly correctly, that the commission of the Confraternity provided for the execution not merely of this predella, but of the altar-piece under which it was to stand. In the year after Uccello left Urbino, Piero della Francesca declined an invitation to complete the altar-piece, and it was not till some years later that Justus of Ghent, a Flemish artist resident at the Urbino court, took up the work and concluded a still extant painting, probably of the same subject and possibly on the same panel as Uccello's, 'The Institution of the Eucharist' (Fig. 16). If Uccello's 'Institution of the Eucharist' was conceived as a formal theorem like the 'Nativity' in San Martino, with a small Christ in the centre of a network of receding lines, it may well have provoked the same censure as another late work, the lost fresco of 'Christ and St. Thomas' over the door of San Tommaso, into which the artist 'put all the study that he knew', and which, when it was unveiled, provoked Donatello to the bitter comment: 'Paolo, you are disclosing it when it should be covered up'.

The style of 'The Profanation of the Host' is that of the backgrounds of the battle-scenes in the National Gallery and the Uffizi. Each figure, reduced to its essential form, is animated by Bosch-like vitality. In work on so reduced a scale there was a premium on literary clarity (an example of this is the silhouetting of the host in the first scene against the black cover of a book), and for this reason profile poses are extensively employed. This 'dry style full of profiles', as it is termed by Vasari, is a feature that was seized on by the artist's imitators, and recurs in a painting of 'Scenes from Monastic Legends' in the Accademia at Florence (Fig. XXXVI) and in a 'Christ on the Cross with four Saints' in the Thyssen collection at Lugano (Fig. XXXIII), sometimes ascribed to Uccello. The use of profile lends the predella at Urbino an adventitious likeness to French miniatures in the following of the Rohan Hours. From the first scene, where a woman redeems her cloak from a Jewish pawnbroker at the price of a consecrated host: through the second, where the Jew and his family, stricken with terror, watch a stream of blood pour from the fire on which the host is placed: the third, in which the host is replaced on an altar by the Pope: the fourth, in which an angel intervenes before the execution of the repentant thief: and the fifth, where the Jew and his family are burned: to the last scene, in which angels and devils dispute over the woman's corpse, the tale is told with a simplicity and an economy of means for which Uccello's earlier work offers no precedent. Linear perspective, where it is employed, is used to create a three-dimensional illusion and not for decorative purposes, and all of the scenes, save the first, are unified by a continuous band

22

16. JUSTUS OF GHENT: THE INSTITUTION OF THE EUCHARIST. *Galleria Nazionale delle Marche, Urbino*

of landscape. This landscape provides a sombre background for the brightly silhouetted figures in the front plane of each episode, and was a sufficiently important element to warrant the reduction of the church shown in the third and sixth scenes to an apse set in the open air. An unfamiliar feature of the predella is the artist's sensibility to tone, as we find it in the first scene in the light flooding through the window on to the right wall, in the third in the mysterious illumination of the distant landscape, and in the fifth where the dresses of the figures grouped round the pyre are lit up by the rising flames.

The recorded payments made to Uccello at Urbino come from the Confraternity of Corpus Domini and not from the court, and there is no proof that he was in the Duke's employment, though he must certainly have come in contact with Laurana and other artists at work in the palace in these years. It is tempting, however, to suppose that in 'The Hunt' in the Ashmolean Museum (Pls. 101–106), the style of which is inseparable from that of 'The Profanation of the Host', we have the remains of a cassone commissioned by Federigo da Montefeltro from Uccello. 'A panel of a hunt by a very ancient and excellent hand', of rather different dimensions,

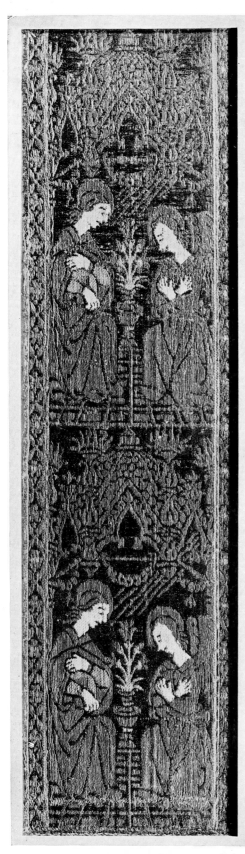

17. THE ANNUNCIATION (woven textile).
Victoria and Albert Museum, London

figures in one of the Urbino inventories. Whether it shows the hounds of the Duke drawing a covert near Urbino or, as another writer has suggested, the young Lorenzo de' Medici hunting in the woods round Pisa, or, as is more likely, a scene from some *novella*, the Oxford 'Hunt', with its scarlet and blue figures beneath dark-green trees, its blue pond fringed with bulrushes and its distant stream, is one of the most unaffectedly romantic paintings of the quattrocento; and it is only gradually (as our eye is drawn inwards by the riding figures to the central triangle in which the stags are rounded up, follows the diminishing figures and the scarlet collars of the hounds, and loses itself in the impenetrable darkness of the wood) that we appreciate the science with which this seemingly artless composition is set out. Whereas in the paintings of Uccello's middle period many of the details are expedients designed to draw attention to the structural skeleton of the design, in this, his latest work, the scheme is so perfectly adjusted that even the device by which the four trees in the foreground divide the panel into three mathematically equal parts is not immediately evident. The orthogonals are marked, less conspicuously than in the battle-pieces, by logs of wood. The lithe silhouettes of the hounds in the foreground of 'The Hunt' are anticipated in the animals that bound across the distance of the battle-scene in the Uffizi, but the smaller scale of the Ashmolean panel gives them a rhythmic impulse of their own. This nervous animation infects the human figures, many of them shown in profile with heads thrown back and open mouths, uttering hunting cries. In some of them, notably the man wearing a violet jerkin to the right of the main group, an element of caricature again suggests the influence of some Flemish or French prototype.

At the end of October or the beginning of November 1468 Uccello returned to Florence. In August 1469 he wrote at the bottom of his tax return: 'I am old and without means of livelihood, my wife is ill and I can no longer work'. 'The Hunt' may thus be not only the latest of his extant paintings but one of his last works. Six years later, on 11 November, Uccello made his will, and on 12 December 1475 (in accordance with instructions he had drawn up half a century before) he was buried in his father's grave at Santo Spirito.

18. FLORENTINE SCHOOL: BATTLE-SCENE. *Museum of Fine Arts, Boston*

Like all great artists, Uccello brought into being imitators of his style. One of these, some-times identified with Dello Delli, was responsible for the frescoes in the bays which intervene between Uccello's earlier and later work in the Chiostro Verde. These frescoes, showing 'Adam and Eve expelled from Paradise and the Labours of Adam and Eve' (Fig. XIX), 'The Sacrifices of Cain and Abel and the Murder of Abel', 'The blind Lamech killing his Great-grandfather and the Building of the Ark' (Fig. XX) and 'The Animals entering the Ark', depend stylistically from the 'Creation' frescoes of Uccello. More puzzling is a cycle of 'Scenes from the Life of the Virgin and the Legend of St. Stephen' painted about 1445 in the Cappella dell'Assunta of the Duomo at Prato by Andrea di Giusto and an artist who is sometimes identified with Uccello (Figs. XXI–XXIII). The rudimentary treat-ment of space throughout these frescoes is not consistent with Uccello's authorship, and the *sinopie* beneath are incompatible in handling with Uccello's, but the figures reveal an artist working in the idiom of the clock-face and of the frescoes at San Miniato. One or two other paintings, among them a Madonna at Dublin (Fig. XXIV) wrongly given to Uccello, can be associated with this hand. Finally, there is a group of smaller paintings, which have some of the characteristics of Uccello's late work and where the sharp profiles and stiff drapery recall the style of the Urbino predella and 'The Hunt'. This group includes one woven textile design (Fig. 17). The only assistant to Uccello of whose name we have a record is a certain Antonio di Papi, who is mentioned in connexion with work at San Miniato al Monte in 1455. Neither in the frescoes in the Chiostro Verde, San Martino alla Scala and the Duomo nor in the Urbino predella is there any trace of studio intervention. In 'The Rout of San Romano', on the other hand, we might expect studio assistance to have been invoked, and the distant figures in the London panel are so far inferior to the Urbino predella and the 'Hunt' as to suggest that they are by a studio hand. An attempt has been made to attribute the Prato frescoes and the works associable with them, to a documented artist, Giovanni di Francesco, to whom the Karlsruhe 'Nativity' and the paintings related to it have also been ascribed. Though the affinities between the Karlsruhe 'Nativity' and the lunette of God the Father with the Holy Innocents painted by Giovanni di Francesco in 1459 for the Spedale degli Innocenti are far from inconsiderable, the two paintings cannot be given to a single hand. The elaborate perspective schemes of 'The Flood' and 'The Nativity' exercised no influence in Florence, for the artists of the generation following Uccello's recog-nized that visual authenticity was best achieved by concealing, not by stressing, the structural mechanism of their designs. Uccello's treatment of the human figure was, however, of some importance for the less controlled, less intellectual style of Andrea del Castagno. More decisive was the appeal which 'The Rout of San Romano' and the Bartolini battle-pieces exerted on the painters of cassone panels (Fig. 18).

Outside Florence, Uccello's relations with Piero della Francesca, his greatest contemporary, form one of the enigmas of the fifteenth century. It may well be that the Urbino 'Flagellation' of Piero, painted about 1455, was influenced by the perspectivism of Uccello, though the architecture in the painting suggests Alberti as the more likely source; it may well be that the visual pattern of 'The Victory of Constantine over Maxentius' at Arezzo derives from 'The Rout of San Romano'; and it may well be that Uccello, in the first panel of the predella at Urbino, was influenced in turn by the luminous surface of the 'Flagellation' and of other paintings by Piero. Despite their common debt to the doctrines of Alberti, the personalities of the two artists are fundamentally diverse; and it is a far cry from Uccello, the inclusive artist animated by ceaseless visual curiosity and unconscious of his limitations or the limitations of his art, to Piero, the exclusive painter whose talent moves majestically forward to its pre-determined close. Uccello's influence over painting in North Italy is problematical. It has been suggested that the lost frescoes in the Casa dei Vitaliani at Padua formed the basis of a drawing by Leonardo da Besozzo in the Crespi-Morbio collection (Fig. XLIII), and are reflected in the Eremitani frescoes of Pizzolo and Mantegna. In so far as the drawings of Leonardo da Besozzo are concerned, this case must be treated with reserve, but we find in Mantegna's frescoes in the Eremitani parallelisms with the later Chiostro Verde frescoes, which may be explained by the assumption either that the two artists, under the common influence of Donatello, were working along somewhat the same lines, or that Mantegna was indebted to Uccello. In either event the perspective technique of Mantegna's frescoes forms a more logical continuation of Uccello's style than any to be found in Florence. For the quattrocento, Uccello's significance far transcends the limits of his direct influence. The 'Hawkwood', in which the resources of a new technique lend substance to the Renaissance ideal of the hero, stands at the head of a long line of equestrian monuments; 'The Flood', in the variety of its gestures and the violence of its emotions, prefigures the 'Battle of Cascina' of Michelangelo; and the perspective of 'The Nativity' is a milestone on the road to the *prospettiva* of Raphael's 'School of Athens'.

The only reputed portrait of Uccello occurs on a panel in the Louvre (Pls. 107–112) along with heads purporting to represent the painter Giotto, the sculptor Donatello, the architect Brunelleschi, and the mathematician Manetti. Though this much-repainted panel has been ascribed to Uccello since the middle of the sixteenth century, the head denominated as Uccello's cannot be regarded with any confidence as a self-portrait. The account of the artist's character given by Vasari, on the other hand, has the ring of authenticity, and we may piece together from the pages of the *Lives* a picture of the artist, 'a shy man . . . solitary, strange, melancholy and poor', his house 'always full of painted representations of birds, cats, dogs, and every sort of strange animal of which he could get drawings, as he was too poor to have the living creatures themselves'; who 'would remain the night long in his study to work out the vanishing points of his perspective' and, when summoned to bed by his wife, replied in the celebrated words: 'How fair a thing is this perspective'. The word 'perspective' recurs like a leitmotiv throughout the narrative. 'Being endowed by nature with a sophistical and subtle disposition, he took pleasure in nothing save in investigating difficult and impossible questions of perspective . . . When engaged upon these matters, Paolo would remain alone in his house

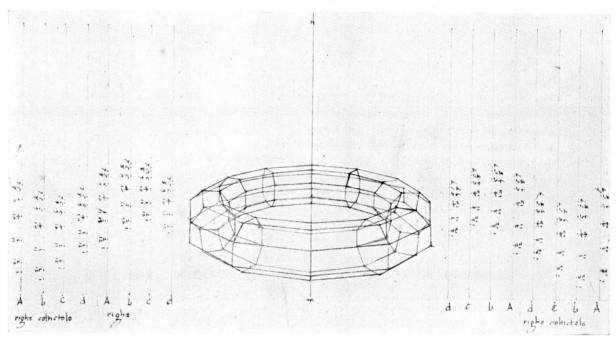

19. PIERO DELLA FRANCESCA: STUDY OF A MAZZOCCHIO FROM THE 'DE PROSPETTIVA PINGENDI'

almost like a hermit, with hardly any intercourse, for weeks and months, not allowing himself to be seen . . . By using up his time on these fancies he remained more poor than famous during his lifetime.' Vasari tells how Donatello, on being shown a number of Uccello's drawings of '*mazzocchi* with projecting points and bosses, represented in perspective from different points of view, spheres with seventy-two facets like diamonds, and on each facet shavings twisted round sticks', retorted with the words: 'Ah, Paolo, this perspective of thine leads thee to abandon the certain for the uncertain; such things are only useful for workers in *intarsia*'. Vasari's insistence on the inutility of these perspective studies, three of which, two showing *mazzocchi* and the third a chalice, survive in the Uffizi (Pls. 85–86), is not wholly warranted, for though they have no practical reference to pictorial composition, they form part of the curriculum of academic perspective, and occur later in the fifteenth century in the *De Prospettiva Pingendi* of Piero della Francesca (Fig. 19) and in the sixteenth century in the *Pratica della Perspettiva* of Daniele Barbaro. It is on these and cognate bodies that Uccello's conversations with Manetti the mathematician must have turned.

From the standpoint of the fifteen-forties appreciation of Uccello demanded a degree of historicity of which Vasari was incapable. How strange the persistence with which Uccello pursued the mathematics of space representation; how perverse the dedication with which he applied himself to theory. Modern criticism has endorsed the verdict of Vasari, that Uccello was a potentially great artist distracted by study of perspective from generating his full force. 'Uccello', writes Berenson, 'had a sense of tactile values and a feeling for colour, but in so far as he used these gifts at all, it was to illustrate scientific problems. His real passion was perspective, and painting was to him a mere occasion for solving some problem in that science, and displaying his mastery over its difficulties.' Another great critic has characterized Uccello as a 'half-artist'. The confusion which has dogged criticism of the painter from Vasari's time down to our own is due in part to misunderstanding of Uccello's contribution to the development of pictorial perspective and in part to abuse of the term

The Decorator and the Naturalist

'science', for his originality is to be sought not in the novelty of his technique, but in the use to which he put it, and the dualism which runs through his work is not between art and science but between two imperfectly reconciled visual traditions and two incompletely synthesized attitudes to art.

Like some settler pressing the area of cultivation on into the bush, Uccello extended the boundaries of painting. Within the context of the fifteenth century he was an innovator intent upon the task of reducing to order the world of visible phenomena, and of containing it, in all its bewildering complexity, within the confines of his picture space. But with the passage of time many of the symbols he employed in the interests of realism have ceased to appear realistic. 'The Flood' requires exposition before it can be understood; the horses in 'The Rout of San Romano' seem inanimate and motionless; and, like the fourth dimension of a fairy tale, the device used for depicting space in 'The Nativity' serves to suspend and not induce belief. Hence there are two Uccellos. One, the more easily perceived today, is a decorator who transports us to the realm of the imagination and builds up a patterned world, where warriors in fantastic plumes struggle in orange groves, and huntsmen, beneath a crescent moon, take part in a nocturnal chase. The other, less readily approachable, is the naturalist of the Chiostro Verde frescoes. And it is this Uccello, aspiring, compassionate and grave, who ranks with the great masters of Italian art.

PLATES

I. THE CREATION OF THE ANIMALS AND THE CREATION OF ADAM; THE CREATION OF EVE AND THE FALL. *Sinopia. Chiostro Verde, S. Maria Novella, Florence*

2. THE CREATION OF THE ANIMALS AND THE CREATION OF ADAM; THE CREATION OF EVE AND THE FALL.
Chiostro Verde, S. Maria Novella, Florence

3. THE CREATION OF THE ANIMALS AND THE CREATION OF ADAM. *Detail of Plate 2*

4. THE CREATION OF EVE AND THE FALL. *Detail of Plate 2*

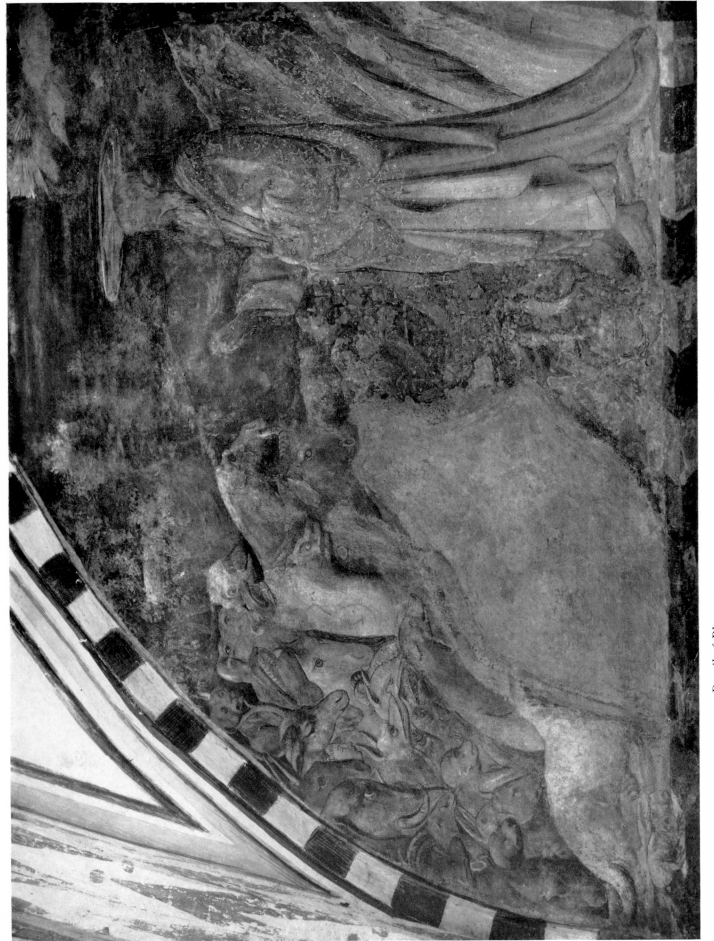

5. THE CREATION OF THE ANIMALS. *Detail of Plate 2*

6. THE CREATION OF ADAM. *Detail of Plate 2*

7. THE ANIMALS. *Detail of Plate 2*

8. ADAM. *Detail of Plate 2*

9. THE FALL. *Detail of Plate 2*

10. THE SERPENT. *Detail of Plate 2*

11. SIR JOHN HAWKWOOD. *Drawing. Gabinetto dei Disegni, Uffizi, Florence*

12. SIR JOHN HAWKWOOD. *Duomo, Florence*

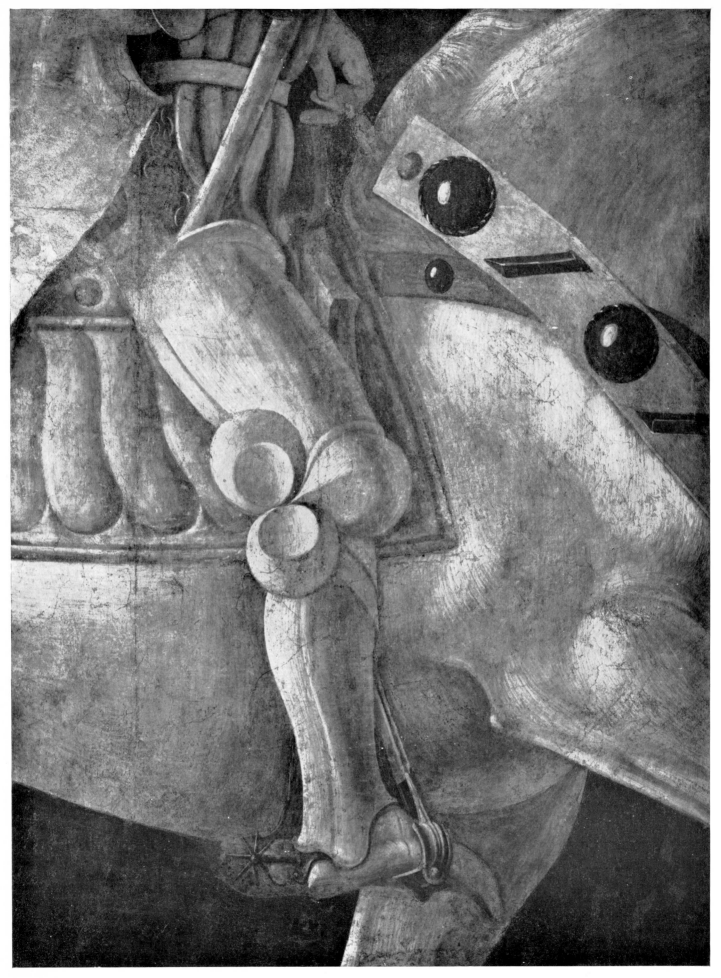

13. SIR JOHN HAWKWOOD. *Detail of Plate 12*

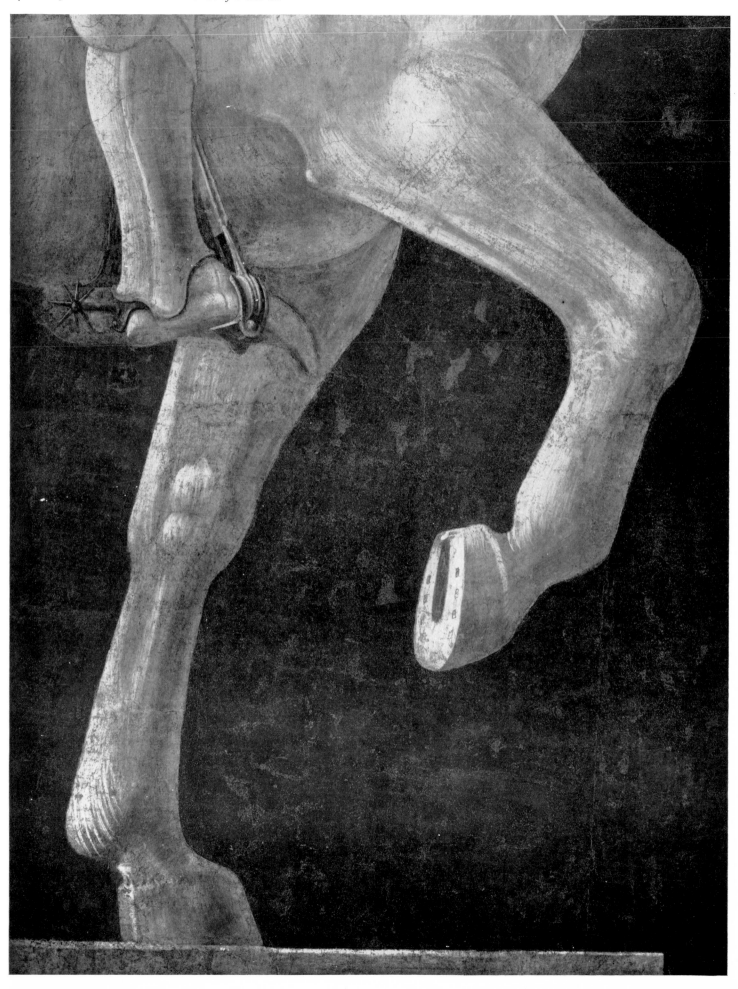

15. SIR JOHN HAWKWOOD. *Detail of Plate 12*

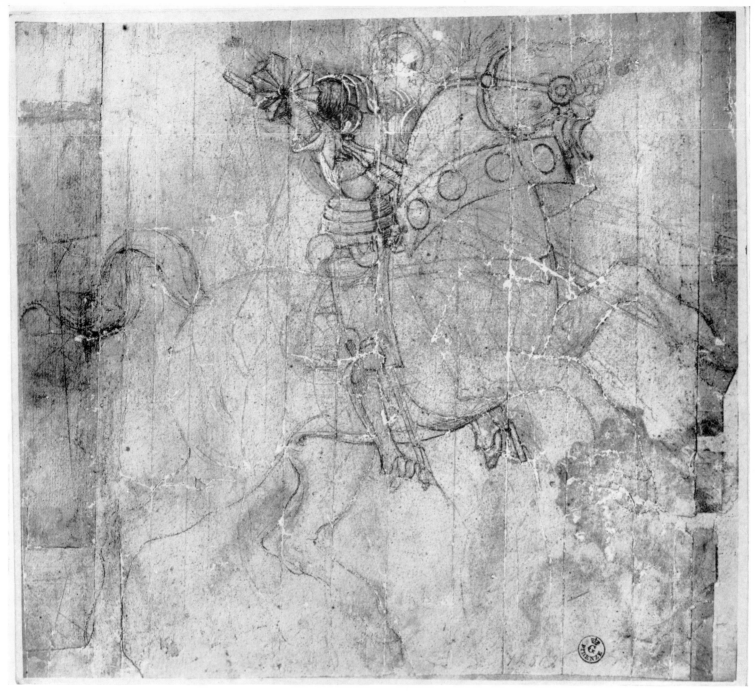

16. A MOUNTED KNIGHT. *Gabinetto dei Disegni, Uffizi, Florence*

17. SCENE FROM THE LEGEND OF A MONASTIC SAINT. S. Miniato al Monte, Florence

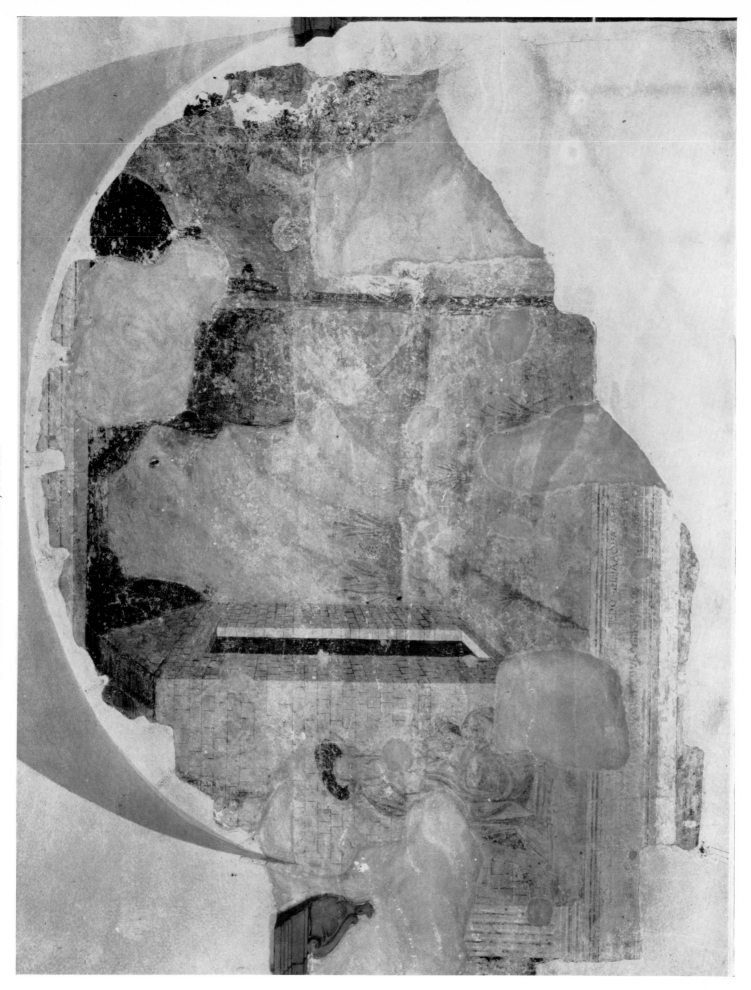

18. SCENE FROM THE LEGEND OF A MONASTIC SAINT. *S. Miniato al Monte, Florence*

19. A MONASTIC SAINT. *Detail of Plate 18*

20. A MONASTIC SAINT. *S. Miniato al Monte, Florence*

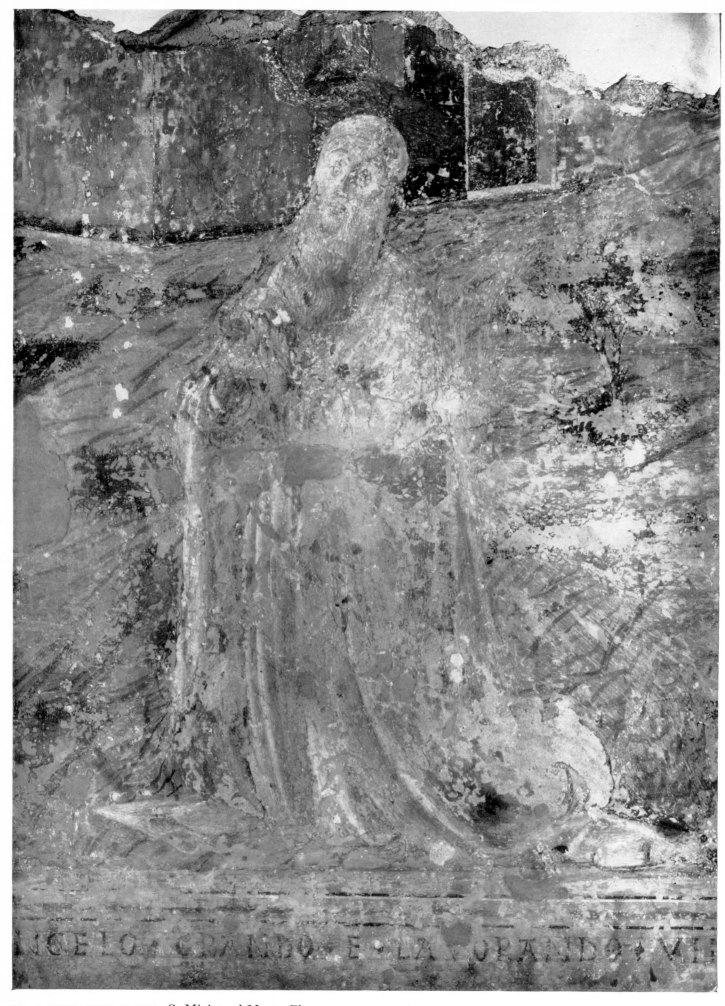

21. A MONASTIC SAINT. *S. Miniato al Monte, Florence*

22. A MONASTIC SAINT. *Detail of Plate 21*

23. AN ANGEL. *S. Miniato al Monte, Florence*

24. AN ANGEL. *Detail of Plate 23*

25. A PROPHET. *Detail of Figure iii. Duomo, Florence*

26. A PROPHET. *Detail of Figure iii. Duomo, Florence*

27. A PROPHET. *Detail of Figure iii. Duomo, Florence*

28. A PROPHET. *Detail of Figure iii. Duomo, Florence*

29. THE NATIVITY. *Stained glass window. Duomo, Florence*

30. THE RESURRECTION. *Stained glass window. Duomo, Florence*

31. THE FLOOD AND THE RECESSION OF THE FLOOD. *Chiostro Verde, S. Maria Novella, Florence*

32. THE SACRIFICE OF NOAH AND THE DRUNKENNESS OF NOAH. *Chiostro Verde, S. Maria Novella, Florence*

33. THE FLOOD. *Detail of Plate 31*

34. THE FLOOD. *Detail of Plate 31*

35. THE RECESSION OF THE FLOOD. *Detail of Plate 31*

36. THE RECESSION OF THE FLOOD. *Detail of Plate 31*

37. THE RECESSION OF THE FLOOD. *Detail of Plate 31*

38. THE FLOOD. *Detail of Plate 31*

39. THE FLOOD. *Detail of Plate 31*

40. THE FLOOD. *Detail of Plate 31*

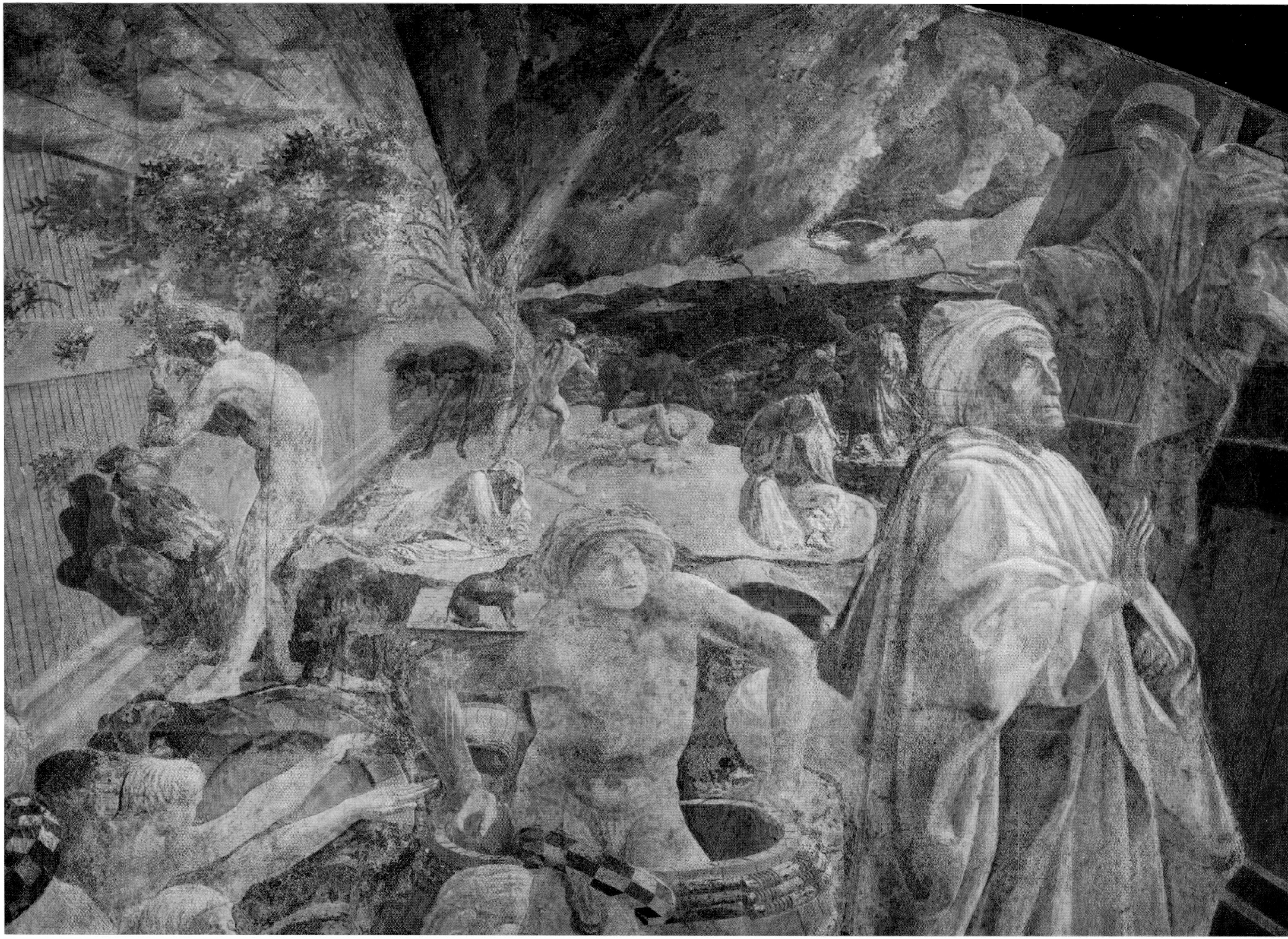

41. THE FLOOD. *Detail of Plate 31*

42. THE FLOOD. *Detail of Plate 31*

43. THE SACRIFICE OF NOAH. *Detail of Plate 32*

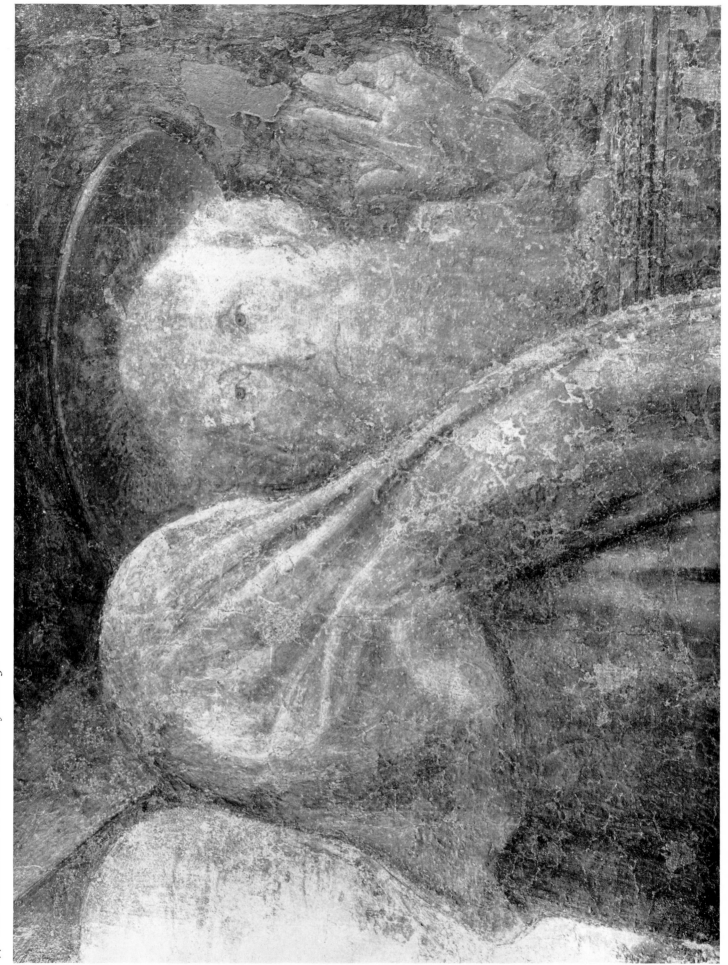

45. THE DRUNKENNESS OF NOAH. *Detail of Plate 32*

46. THE DRUNKENNESS OF NOAH. *Detail of Plate 32*

47. THE DRUNKENNESS OF NOAH. *Detail of Plate 32*

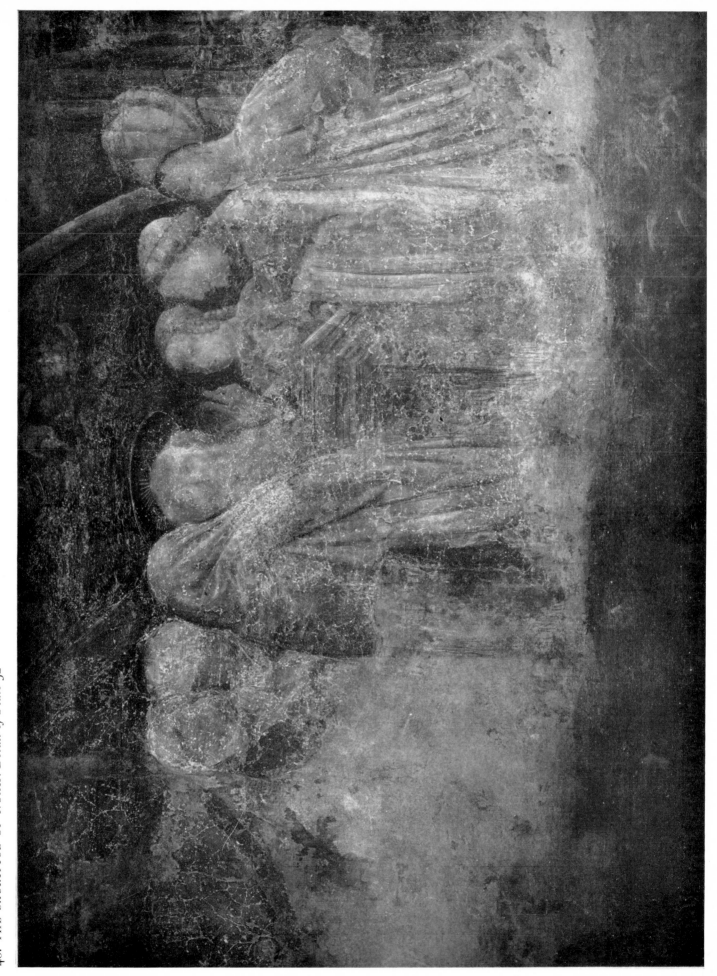

48. THE SACRIFICE OF NOAH. *Detail of Plate 32*

49. PORTRAIT OF A YOUNG MAN. *Musée Benoit-Molin, Chambéry*

50. MALE HEAD IN LEFT PROFILE. *Drawing. Gabinetto dei Disegni, Uffizi, Florence*

57. THE ROUT OF SAN ROMANO. *Detail of Plate 51*

58. THE ROUT OF SAN ROMANO. *Detail of Plate 51*

59. THE ROUT OF SAN ROMANO. *Detail of Plate 51*

61. THE ROUT OF SAN ROMANO. *Uffizi, Florence*

63. THE ROUT OF SAN ROMANO. *Details of Plate 61*

64. THE ROUT OF SAN ROMANO. *Detail of Plate 61*

65. THE ROUT OF SAN ROMANO. *Detail of Plate 61*

66. THE ROUT OF SAN ROMANO. *Detail of Plate 61*

67. THE ROUT OF SAN ROMANO. *Detail of Plate 61*

71. THE ROUT OF SAN ROMANO. *Louvre, Paris*

72. THE ROUT OF SAN ROMANO. *Detail of Plate 71*

73. THE ROUT OF SAN ROMANO. *Detail of Plate 71*

74. THE ROUT OF SAN ROMANO. *Detail of Plate 71*

75. THE ROUT OF SAN ROMANO. *Detail of Plate 71*

76. THE ROUT OF SAN ROMANO. *Detail of Plate 71*

77. SAINT GEORGE AND THE DRAGON. *Musée Jacquemart-André, Paris*

79. SAINT GEORGE AND THE DRAGON. *Detail of Plate 77*

80. SAINT GEORGE AND THE DRAGON. *Detail of Plate 78*

81. SAINT GEORGE AND THE DRAGON. *Detail of Plate 78*

82. SAINT GEORGE AND THE DRAGON. *Detail of Plate 78*

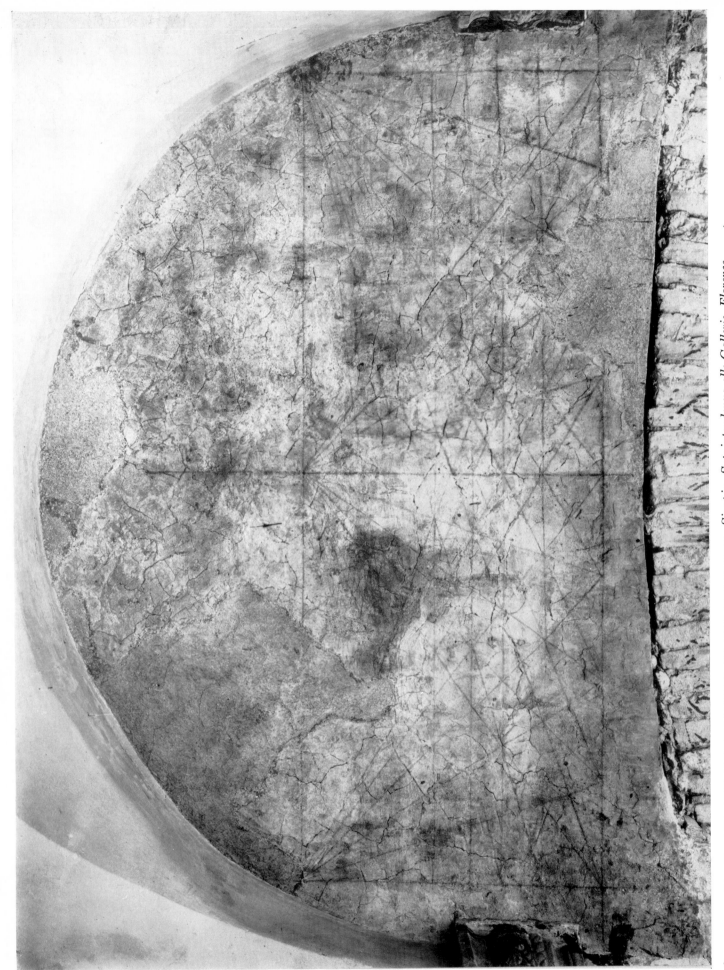

83. THE NATIVITY AND THE ANNUNCIATION TO THE SHEPHERDS. *Sinopia. Soprintendenza alle Gallerie, Florence*

84. THE NATIVITY AND THE ANNUNCIATION TO THE SHEPHERDS. *Soprintendenza alle Gallerie, Florence*

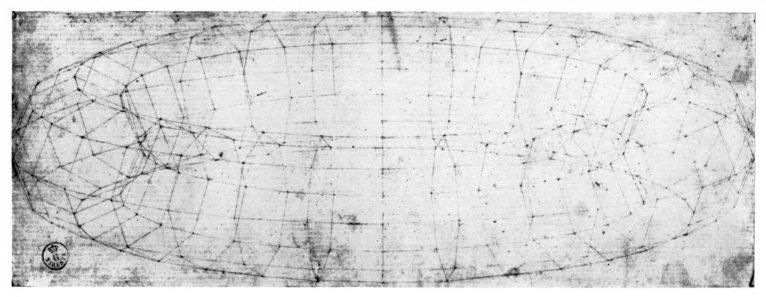

85a. PERSPECTIVE STUDY OF A MAZZOCCHIO. *Drawing. Gabinetto dei Disegni, Uffizi, Florence*

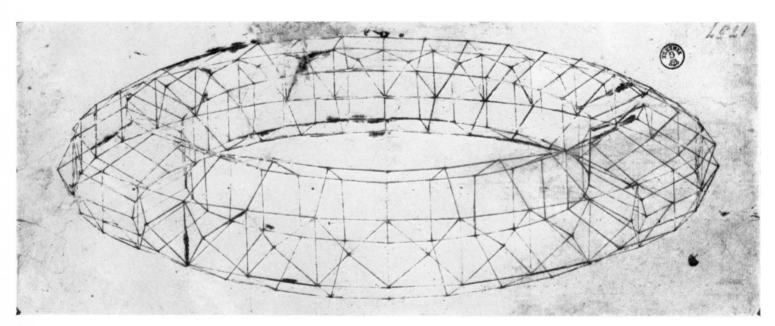

85b. PERSPECTIVE STUDY OF A MAZZOCCHIO. *Drawing. Gabinetto dei Disegni, Uffizi, Florence*

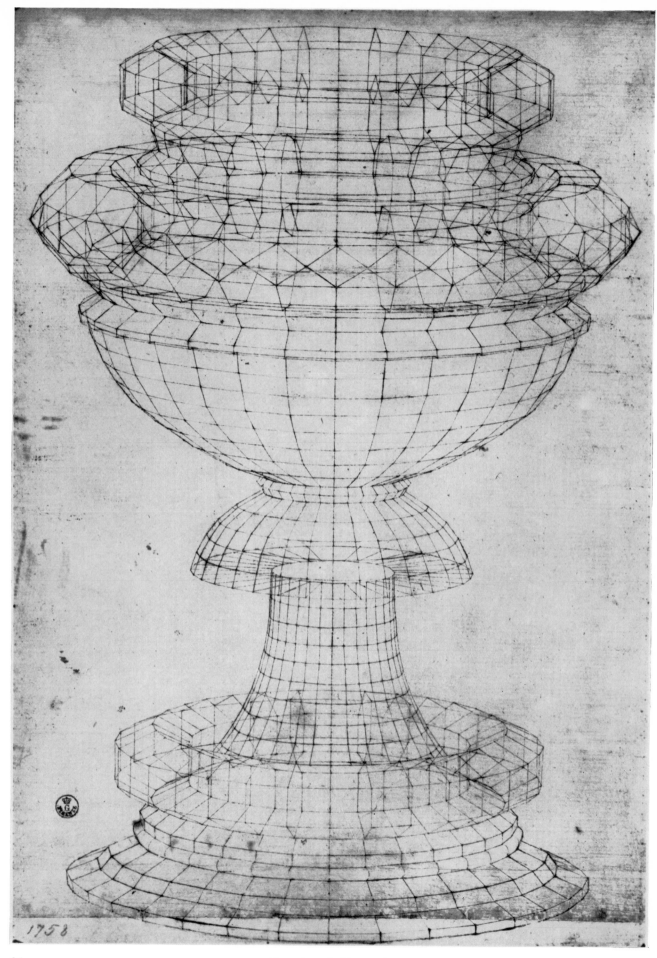

1758

86. PERSPECTIVE STUDY OF A CHALICE. *Drawing. Gabinetto dei Disegni, Uffizi, Florence*

87–89. THE PROFANATION OF THE HOST. *Galleria Nazionale delle Marche, Urbino*
A woman redeems her cloak at the price of a consecrated Host
The attempted destruction of the Host
The Host restored to the altar

90–92. THE PROFANATION OF THE HOST. *Galleria Nazionale delle Marche, Urbino*
The execution of the repentant woman
The Jew and his family are burned
Angels and devils dispute over the woman's corpse

93. A WOMAN REDEEMS HER CLOAK AT THE PRICE OF A CONSECRATED HOST. *Detail of Plate 87*

94. INTERIOR OF A ROOM. *Detail of Plate 87*

95. THE FAMILY OF THE JEW. *Detail of Plate 88*

96. THE PROCESSION TO THE ALTAR. *Detail of Plate 89*

97. HORSEMEN. *Detail of Plate 90*

98. HORSEMEN. *Detail of Plate 91*

99. THE EXECUTION OF THE REPENTANT WOMAN. *Detail of Plate 90*

100. THE JEW AND HIS FAMILY ARE BURNED. *Detail of Plate 91*

101. A HUNT. *Ashmolean Museum, Oxford*

102. A HUNT. *Detail of Plate 101*

103. A HUNT. *Detail of Plate 101*

105. A HUNT. *Detail of Plate 101*

106. A HUNT. *Detail of Plate 101*

107. THE FOUNDERS OF FLORENTINE ART. *Louvre, Paris*

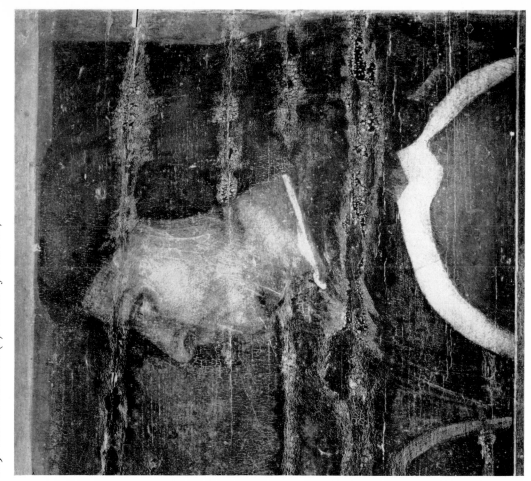

109. BRUNELLESCHI(?). *Detail of Plate 107*

108. GIOTTO(?). *Detail of Plate 107*

110. DONATELLO(?). *Detail of Plate 107*

III. ANTONIO MANETTI(?). *Detail of Plate 107*

112. PAOLO UCCELLO(?). *Detail of Plate 107*

CATALOGUE

CATALOGUE

THE CREATION OF THE ANIMALS and THE CREATION OF ADAM; THE CREATION OF EVE and THE FALL
Chiostro Verde, Sta Maria Novella, Florence.

PLATES 1–10

Fresco (transferred). Upper scene 210×452 cm. Lower scene 244×478 cm.

The construction of the Chiostro Verde (Green Cloister), between the church of Sta Maria Novella and the Great Cloister of the convent, appears to have been begun about 1350 (Wood Brown, *The Dominican Church of Santa Maria Novella at Florence*, 1902, p. 84) and to have been completed by 1359. Under the will of Turino Baldese of 22 July 1348, the convent had received the sum of one thousand lire to defray the expenses of painting a cycle of scenes from the Old Testament, and it is suggested by Campani ('Uccello's Story of Noah in the Chiostro Verde', in *The Burlington Magazine*, xvii, 1910, p. 203) that this fund was applied to the decoration of the new cloister. It is sometimes assumed (Crowe and Cavalcaselle, *A History of Painting in Italy*, ed. Langton Douglas and De Nicola, iv, 1911, p. 124n.) that the cloister was decorated with grisaille frescoes in the fourteenth century, and that these were later replaced by the existing frescoes; there is, however, no evidence of this, and neither the 'Scenes from the Story of Abraham' on the south wall of the cloister, ascribed by Pudelko ('The Minor Masters of the Chiostro Verde', in *The Art Bulletin*, xvii, 1935, pp. 76–83) with some plausibility to the Master of the Bargello Tondo, nor those on the west wall, ascribed by Pudelko (op. cit., pp. 83–9) to the pseudo-Ambrogio Baldese, can have been executed before the end of the first or the beginning of the second quarter of the fifteenth century. It is likely that the decoration of the south and west walls of the cloister preceded that of the east wall, on which the frescoes associable with Uccello are set. The bays of the east wall, like those of the south and west walls, are divided horizontally into two areas, that below an oblong rectangle and that above a lunette. Reading from the north-eastern corner of the cloister, the bays on the east wall represent: (i) above, 'The Creation of the Animals' and 'The Creation of Adam', below, 'The Creation of Eve' and 'The Fall of Adam and Eve'; (ii) above, 'The Expulsion from Paradise' and 'The later Life of Adam and Eve', below, 'The Sacrifices of Cain and Abel' and 'The Murder of Abel'; (iii) above, 'The blind Lamech kills his Great-Grandfather' and 'The Building of the Ark', below, 'The Entry of the Animals into the Ark'; (iv) above, 'The Flood' and 'The Recession of the Flood', below, 'The Sacrifice of Noah' and 'The Drunkenness of Noah'; (v) 'The Building of the Tower of Babel' (almost totally erased); (vi) subjects indecipherable. Of these frescoes those in bays (i) and (iv) are by Uccello, those in bays (ii) and (iii) are by an Uccellesque artist

who is identified by Pudelko (op. cit., pp. 72–6) with Dello Delli, and that in bay (v) is by an archaizing hand, perhaps that of the artist responsible for the bulk of the scenes on the west wall.

There is a remarkable degree of unanimity among early sources in attributing the frescoes in the first bay to Uccello, under whose name they appear in the *Operette istoriche di Antonio Manetti* (ed. Milanesi, 1887, pp. 167–8), the *Memoriale* of Albertini of 1510 (*Il Memoriale di Francesco Albertini*, cura Herberti P. Horne, 1909, p. 14: 'Nel primo claustro sono hystorie antique: la prima di Adam et Eua, et quella di Noe per mano di Paulo Vccelli'), the *Libro di Antonio Billi* of 1516–25/30 (*Il Libro di Antonio Billi*, herausgegeben von Carl Frey, 1892, p. 25: 'Fecie nel primo chiostro di Santa Maria Nouella una storia, quando Dio plasmo Adamo et Eua, et come loro furono cacciati dal paradiso delle delitie, et una storia del diluuio, cose bellissime'), the rather later Anonimo Magliabechiano (*Il Codice Magliabechiano*, herausgegeben von Carl Frey, 1892, p. 99, in a passage deriving from the *Libro di Antonio Billi*), and Vasari (*Vite*, ed. Milanesi, ii, 1906, pp. 208–9: 'Gli fu fatto poi allogagione, nel chiostro di Santa Maria Novella, d'alcune storie; le prime delle quali sono, quando s'entra in chiesa nel chiostro, la creazione degli animali . . . Fecevi la creazione dell'uomo e della femmina, ed il peccar loro, con bella maniera, affaticata e ben condotta . . . Finito ch'ebbe questo, lavoro nel medesimo chiostro, sotto due storie di mano d'altri, e piu basso fece il Diluvio, con l'arca di Noe . . . Sotto questa storia dipinse ancora l'inebriazione di Noe'). The traditional attribution to Uccello is accepted *inter alios* by Crowe and Cavalcaselle (op. cit., pp. 115–17), Berenson (*Italian Paintings of the Renaissance*, 1932, p. 582, and subsequent editions, omitted from earlier editions of *The Florentine Painters of the Renaissance*), Salmi (*Paolo Uccello, Andrea del Castagno, Domenico Veneziano*, 1938, pp. 11–14), Lionello Venturi ('Paolo Uccello', in *L'Arte*, xxxiii, 1930, p. 63), Pudelko ('The Early Works of Paolo Uccello', in *The Art Bulletin*, xvi, 1934, pp. 237–43), Paatz ('Una Natività di Paolo Uccello e alcune considerazioni sull'arte del Maestro', in *Rivista d'Arte*, xvi, 1934, p. 118), Pittaluga (*Paolo Uccello*, 1946, pp. 9–10) and Meiss (cited by Krautheimer, *Lorenzo Ghiberti*, 1956, p. 209). The two frescoes are attributed by Longhi ('Ricerche su Giovanni di Francesco' in *Pinacoteca*, i, 1928, p. 36) and Fiocco ('Dello Delli scultore', in *Rivista d'Arte*, xi, 1920, p. 42) to Dello Delli, and by Van Marle (*Development of the Italian Schools of Painting*, x, 1928, p. 226) to 'the hand of a praiseworthy pupil', and are omitted from the Uccello catalogue of Boeck (*Paolo Uccello*, 1939, p. 118). A dating 'prior to Uccello's journey to Venice in 1425' is postulated by Horne ('Andrea del Castagno', in *The Burlington Magazine*, vii, 1905, p. 229) and Borsook (*The Mural Painters of Tuscany*, 1960, p. 148). Salmi (loc. cit.) places the frescoes about

1431, after Uccello's return to Florence, and Pudelko (op. cit., p. 243) localizes them in the bracket 1430–6. They are dated in the early fourteen-thirties by Micheletti (in *Mostra di quattro maestri del primo rinascimento*, 1954, p. 26), Berti (in *Affreschi staccati*, 1957, nos. 63–4, and *Affreschi staccati: II Mostra*, 1958, nos. 34–7) and Sindona (*Paolo Uccello*, 1957, pp. 29 f., 58). The formal connexion between the figure of Eve in the lower fresco and the Christ in the window of the 'Resurrection' of 1443 supports a dating in the mid-thirties immediately before the 'Hawkwood'. Undue importance has been attached to the absence of perspective features in the upper scene, and Horne (loc. cit.) alone stresses the significance of the parti-coloured string-course dividing the two frescoes, which recurs in a less accurate form in the two following bays. Like all of the frescoes on the east wall of the cloister, the two scenes have been seriously damaged as a result of the disintegration of the wall surface. This is attributed by Wood Brown (op. cit., p. 96) to the fact that the east wall of the cloister is a retaining wall. Both frescoes were removed from the wall in 1940 and subjected to superficial cleaning. They were exhibited in this state in 1954 in the *Mostra di quattro maestri del primo rinascimento* (Palazzo Strozzi, Florence) and were cleaned again between this date and 1957, when they were shown in the *Mostra di affreschi staccati* (Fortezza di Belvedere, Florence). As with the later frescoes painted by Uccello in the cloister, the removal of the paint film brought to light the underlying *sinopie* drawn by the artist in red on the whitewashed surface of the wall. It has been suggested that the handling of these cartoons is inconsistent with that of the cartoon discovered beneath 'The Drunkenness of Noah'; in practice the style of the cartoons serves to confirm rather than disprove the ascription to Uccello of the earlier scenes. Procacci (*Sinopie e affreschi*, 1960, p. 64 f.) argues from the *sinopie* that the two frescoes were designed and drawn out on the wall by Uccello at the same time as 'The Drunkenness of Noah' and 'The Flood', but were executed by a member of the artist's shop. This theory is based on the employment in the figure of God the Father in 'The Creation of Adam' of a technique (*spolvero*) for transferring the preliminary drawing to the wall which was not in general use before the middle of the century. The view that the *sinopie* of the two sets of frescoes date from the same time is inconsistent with the style of the cartoons themselves, while the theory that the present frescoes are due to an assistant of Uccello, not to the master, is contradicted by their elevated figure style. The cartoon is essential to an understanding of the lower scene, since the figure of Adam in 'The Creation of Eve' and the lower part of the coiled serpent in 'The Fall' are wholly or virtually obliterated in the fresco, and the figures of God the Father and Eve on the left are less readily visible than in the *sinopia*. The tonality of the fresco is determined by the *terra verde* in which the greater part is executed, and by the dull red background; traces of local colour are found in the blue and red flowers sprinkled across the green grass on the right, in the yellow round the

neck and across the shoulder of the robe of God the Father, and in the yellow perspective haloes. Among the many restored passages visible in photographs made before 1957 may be noted especially areas of repaint in the left leg and left forearm of Adam in the upper fresco, and on the cheek of the serpent below. Like the comparable figure on Ghiberti's Gate of Paradise, the Adam in 'The Creation of Adam' depends from a classical model of the class of the Rospigliosi Adonis (for this see Krautheimer, op. cit., p. 344). It is established by Krautheimer that motifs from the second bronze door were known to Uccello before the door itself was cast, perhaps in the form of drawings or preliminary models supplied by Ghiberti for Uccello's use.

SIR JOHN HAWKWOOD
Duomo, Florence.
PLATES 12–15

Fresco transferred to canvas. Inscribed on the tomb-chest IOANNES·ACVTVS·EQVES BRITANNICVS·DVX· AETATIS·S/VAE CAVTISSIMVS·ET·REI·MILITARIS PERITISSIMVS·HABITVS EST, and on the frieze of the supporting platform ·PAVLI·VCELLI·OPVS.

The story of the monument to Sir John Hawkwood (d. 1394) goes back to the year preceding the great condottiere's death, when on 20 August provision was made by the Operaii of the Duomo for 'unam honorabilem et magnificam sepolturam . . . in qua possit recondi corpus ipsius domini Johannis quando morietur'. This monument was to be 'ornari lapidibus et figuris marmoriis' (see Poggi, 'Paolo Uccello e l'orologio di S. Maria del Fiore', in *Miscellanea di storia dell'arte in onore di Igino Benvenuto Supino*, 1933, pp. 330–4, for full texts of this and the following documents). On May 16 of the following year, after Hawkwood's death, the tomb was walled up, and on 2 December 1395 it was agreed that monuments to Hawkwood and to the condottiere Piero Farnese should be designed by the painters Agnolo Gaddi and Giuliano d'Arrigo for a site 'inter duas januas versus viam capsettariorum'. The two artists mentioned in this document had been responsible five years earlier for designing a wooden equestrian statue of Piero Farnese (Salvini, *L'Arte di Agnolo Gaddi*, 1936, p. 181), 'que iam antiqua et non apparens est, et in loco non apta posita'. Subsequent references indicate that the proposed monument took the form, not of a marble tomb as had been originally intended, but of a fresco, presumably executed by the two artists named in the document of 1395. No further reference to the Hawkwood monument occurs till 1433, when in March it was put out by the Operaii to open competition. Three years later it was decided that the matter must be expedited, and on 30 May Uccello was instructed to replace the existing fresco with a new fresco *de terra viridi*. On 28 June, however, it was ordered that the horse and rider executed by Uccello as a result of this instruction, should be effaced 'quia non est pictus ut decet', and on 6 July, Uccello was instructed to make a second attempt. A document of 31 August implies that by that time the fresco was complete, and Uccello received payment for both the earlier and the later versions. On 17 December 1436, it was enjoined that the lettering of the inscription on the sarcophagus should be revised. A companion fresco of Niccolò da Tolentino (d. 1435) was painted by Andrea del Castagno in 1456. Both frescoes were restored in 1524 by Lorenzo di Credi (Vasari, *Vite*, ed. Milanesi, iv, p. 568n.). Salmi (*Paolo Uccello, Andrea del Castagno, Domenico Veneziano*, 1938, p. 138), interpreting the record of this transaction in a literal sense, assumes that restoration was limited to the horses of the two frescoes, while Reymond ('L'architecture des peintres aux premières années de la Renaissance', in *Revue de l'Art*, xvii, 1905, p. 41) refers the document to the painted frames. In any event the painted border of the 'Hawkwood' must date from the early sixteenth century, and is thus an accretion to Uccello's scheme. According to Baldinucci (*Notizie dei Professori del Disegno*, iii, 1768, p. 125), the fresco was again restored in 1688. In 1842 it was removed from the wall and transferred to canvas, and for more than a century thereafter hung on the west wall of the church (for this see Paatz, *Die Kirchen von Florenz*, iii, 1952, pp. 369, 419, 491–3). In 1947 it was replaced on the north wall. The fresco has been seriously impaired by the vicissitudes which it has undergone, and Boeck (*Paolo Uccello*, 1939, p. 112) notes that no trace now remains of a shadow represented in an engraving published by Caulfield in 1793 as cast by the riding figure against the wall. Though the damage is less general than is suggested by Marangoni ('Osservazioni sull' Acuto di Paolo Uccello', in *L'Arte*, xxii, 1919, pp. 37 ff.), the head in particular is much abraded. For Longhi (*Piero della Francesca*, 1947, p. 157) the horse in its present form is consistent with Uccello's style of about 1455, and must therefore have been repainted by the artist at the time when Castagno was engaged on the 'Niccolò da Tolentino'. This view is supported by Carli (*Tutta la pittura di Paolo Uccello*, 2nd. ed., 1959, pp. 17, 54). The fresco was cleaned in 1953–4.

The effigy is justly described by Berti (*Paolo Uccello*, No. 29 in *I Maestri del Colore*, 1964) as 'la seconda esemplificazione del nuovo sistema prospettico in pittura, dieci anni dopo la *Trinita* di Masaccio'. A conjectural reconstruction of the system of projection employed in it is given by Gioseffi ('Complementi di prospettiva, 2: di un nuovo libro; di Apollodoro d'Atene; di Filippo, di Paolo e d'altri', in *Critica d'Arte*, v, 1958, pp. 131).

SIR JOHN HAWKWOOD

Uffizi, Florence (Gabinetto dei Disegni, No. 31F).

PLATE 11

Silverpoint heightened in white on a prepared light green ground: background dull red. 46×33 cm. Squared with a stylus.

Berenson, *The Drawings of the Florentine Painters*, i, 1938, No. 2767, p. 14: 'It is in a lamentable condition, and is now of small value. In its original state it

probably differed in no detail from the fresco, and at present, far from throwing any light on the genesis of this work, it needs the painting for its interpretation. Only in the horse's tail is there still a quality of movement and of line that reveals the master.' This extreme view is rejected by Marangoni ('Osservazioni sull' Acuto di Paolo Uccello', in *L'Arte*, xxii, 1919, pp. 37 ff.) and Pudelko ('The Early Works of Paolo Uccello', in *The Art Bulletin*, xvi, 1934, p. 233), the latter claiming that 'the thorough restoration undergone by the fresco in the course of the last century makes it easier to understand Uccello's intentions from the study in the Uffizi'. The principal compositional difference between the drawing and fresco is in the relation of the rear foot of the horse to the left edge of the sarcophagus. It is pointed out by Schmitt ('Paolo Uccellos Entwurf für das Reiterbild des Hawkwood,' in *Mitteilungen des Kunsthistorischen Institutes in Florenz*, 1959, pp. 125 ff.) and Borsook (*The Mural Painters of Tuscany*, 1960, p. 149) that the drawing has been torn and incorrectly repaired. When the drawing was intact, it would have corresponded exactly with the fresco. Borsook (loc. cit.) describes this as 'the earliest squared drawing in existence'. This is correct, though there is evidence (for which see Oertel, 'Wandmalerei und Zeichnung in Italien', in *Mitteilungen des Kunsthistorischen Institutes in Florenz*, v, 1937–40, pp. 303–5) that a system of squaring was employed in the Masaccio 'Trinity'. There is no confirmation of Pudelko's view that the sarcophagus in the fresco was shortened in the course of restoration. Marangoni notes that the geometrical character of the horse in the drawing is lost in the fresco, and attributes this to 'grossolani e disastrosi rifacimenti posteriori', perhaps carried out in 1688. These geometrical forms are the main feature distinguishing the drawing from the fresco.

A MOUNTED KNIGHT

Uffizi, Florence (Gabinetto dei Disegni, No. 14502F).

PLATE 16

Black chalk with white heightening on turquoise or greenish prepared paper (squared): 30×33 cm.

Berenson (*The Drawings of the Florentine Painters*, 1938, No. 2769) as Uccello. The unanimity with which this splendid drawing is ascribed to Uccello is not accompanied by agreement as to the purpose for which it was made. Salmi (*Paolo Uccello, Andrea del Castagno, Domenico Veneziano*, 1938, p. 24) and other critics interpret the figure as a St. George, and Sindona (*Paolo Uccello*, 1957, p. 38) links it tentatively with the 'St. George and the Dragon' in London. Popham (*Italian Drawings exhibited at the Royal Academy, Burlington House, London*, 1931, p. 9, No. 29) regards it tentatively as a study for a horseman in 'The Rout of San Romano'. The fact that the drawing is pricked and squared for enlargement renders it likely that the study was utilized in some larger composition, perhaps, as suggested by Berenson (op. cit., i, p. 15), the lost battle-pieces painted by Uccello for the Casa Bartolini.

Catalogue

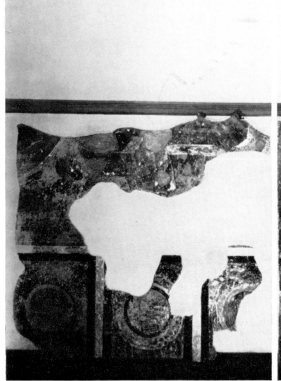

I. FLORENTINE SCHOOL: SCENES FROM MONASTIC LEGENDS. *San Miniato al Monte, Florence*

SCENES FROM MONASTIC LEGENDS
San Miniato al Monte, Florence.
PLATES 17–24; Figs. I, II-a, II-b.

The fresco cycle in the cloister of San Miniato al Monte is mentioned as a work of Uccello by Albertini (*Memoriale di molte statue e pitture della citta di Firenze fatto da Francesco Albertini*, 1863, p. 17: 'Nel primo claustro di sopra sono XII quadri di Paulo Uccello'). Vasari (ed. cit., ii, p. 207) states that Uccello 'lavoro anco in San Miniato fuor di Fiorenza in un chiostro, di verdeterra ed in parte colorito, le vite de' santi Padri: nelle quali non osservo molto l'unione di fare d'un solo colore, come si deono, le storie; perche fece i campi azzurri, le citta di color rosso, e gli edificj variati secondo che gli parve: ed in questo manco, perche le cose che si fingono di pietra, non possono e non deono essere tinte d'altro colore'. The frescoes were whitewashed in the seventeenth or eighteenth century, and remained unknown till their discovery in 1925 by Marangoni, by whom the more important of them were published ('Gli affreschi di Paolo Uccello a San Miniato a Firenze', in *Rivista d'Arte*, xii, 1930, pp. 403–17). A further fresco and a contiguous fragment, disclosed in 1942, are reproduced by Salmi ('Riflessioni su Paolo Uccello', in *Commentari*, i, 1950, pp. 23–6).

Reading from right to left the frescoes show: (i) a bearded monk (usually identified as St. Benedict) seated on the left against the grey wall of a church or monastery instructing an almost obliterated figure

II-a. FLORENTINE SCHOOL: SCENE FROM THE LIFE OF A HERMIT. *San Miniato al Monte, Florence*

11-b. FLORENTINE SCHOOL: VISION OF A HERMIT. *San Miniato al Monte, Florence*

standing on the right beside a tree to pour away the liquid (usually described as poisoned wine) contained in an amphora or jar; (ii) a monk seated beside a river in a hilly landscape; (iii) a monk seated on the left with left hand raised in astonishment at a golden dish proffered by an angel or other obliterated figure to his right; (iv) a bearded monk kneeling on the left accosted by an angel in left profile, above the inscription (APAREN)DOGLI. L. ANGELO. ORANDO. VINSE. PE(RF)ETAMENTE (L)ACIDIA.; (v) an almost erased scene, in which the centre is occupied by a table and part of the figure of a monk can be seen on the right, above an illegible inscription; (vi) a fragmentary head of a monk in *terra verde*; (vii) a seated or kneeling monk in the left foreground, on the right a flight of pink steps and a group of *terra verde* figures. There appear originally to have been eight frescoes on the east wall, divided by painted pilasters. Salmi (loc. cit.) assumes that the series ran to the north end of the east wall, and that it therefore consisted of nine scenes; there is no explicit evidence to support this not untenable view. Beneath each fresco were three rectangles containing round bosses. Only the frescoes listed as (i) and (vii) above retain their original height; it is clear that like the somewhat similar frescoes in the cloister of the Badia each originally had an arched top.

The decoration of the south wall (Figs. 11-a, 11-b) is now limited to two scenes in one of which a youthful male figure (reduced to the red under-drawing), turned to the right, raises one hand in astonishment at a vision of God the Father supported by seraphim which appears to a monk kneeling outside a cave; two ravens are seen on the ground. At the west end of the wall a monk wearing a halo is seen approaching a door; to the right a kneeling monk or cenobite, also with a halo, kneels inside a grey cave. An indication of the subjects of the scenes represented on this wall (in which the fresco strip was evidently shallower than on the east wall) is afforded by the inscription QVARTA GENERATIONE DEI CENOBITI ORATORI on the first fresco.

The scenes on the east wall are given to Uccello by all earlier writers, including Berenson, who at one time (*Pitture italiane del Rinascimento*, 1936, p. 271) ascribed them to the Carrand Master, but who later (*Italian Pictures of the Renaissance: Florentine School*, 1963, p. 203) accepted them as fragmentary early works by Uccello. Boeck (*Paolo Uccello*, 1939, pp. 23–8) wrongly regards the frescoes on the south side of the cloister as by the same hand as those on the east wall. This view is endorsed by Procacci (*Sinopie e affreschi*, 1960, p. 39). The frescoes on the east wall are dated by Marangoni, Pudelko ('The Early Works of Paolo Uccello', in *The Art Bulletin*, xvi, 1934, p. 243), Pittaluga (*Paolo Uccello*, 1946, p. 13), Procacci (*Mostra di affreschi staccati*, 1957, p. 56) and Carli (*Tutta la pittura di Paolo Uccello*, 2nd ed., 1959, pp. 54–5) about 1440. Salmi (*Paolo Uccello, Andrea del Castagno, Domenico Veneziano*, 1938, pp. 21, 139–40) regards them as prior to 1439; Sindona (*Paolo Uccello*, 1957, pp. 28, 58) places them soon after Uccello's return from Venice in 1430; and Boeck proposes a dating about 1425. A

dating about 1440 was accepted in the first edition of this book. It has since been proved by Saalman ('Paolo Uccello at San Miniato', in *Burlington Magazine*, cvi, 1964, pp. 558–63) that the cloister in which the frescoes were painted was constructed between 1442 and 1447, and that the walls cannot have been decorated before the latter year. The frescoes on the east wall of the cloister are somewhat different in style from the later Chiostro Verde frescoes ('The Flood' and 'The Drunkenness of Noah') and can be regarded as Uccello's only if they were painted in an antecedent phase. A document published by Saalman shows that a certain Giovanni Schiavo (perhaps identical with Giovanni di Francesco) was paid for painting in the cloister in 1448.

CLOCK FACE
Duomo, Florence.
PLATES 25–8

Vasari (ed. cit., ii, pp. 212–13), after describing the 'Hawkwood', states that Uccello 'fece nel medesimo tempo e nella medesima chiesa, di colorito, la sfera dell'ore sopra alla porta principale dentro la chiesa, con quattro teste ne' canti colorite in fresco'. Documents published by Poggi ('Paolo Uccello e l'orologio di Santa Maria del Fiore', in *Miscellanea di storia dell'arte in onore di Igino Benvenuto Supino*, 1933, pp. 323–36) enable this work to be localized in the first half of 1443, when Uccello received on 22 February a payment for work on the clock and on 2 April a further payment 'pro dorando stellam oriuoli et pro dorando unam pallam in punta razi, et pro remuneratione sui laboris in mictendo d'azuro campum ubi manet stella'. Situated at the west end of the Cathedral, the clock was supplied with a modern face in the nineteenth century. Cleaning undertaken in 1963–8 (for which see U. Baldini, 'L'orologio di Paolo Uccello,' in *La Nazione*, 6 December, 1968, p. 10) resulted in the recovery of the original clock-face. This is divided into twenty-four sections with Roman numerals running in an anti-clockwise direction from the base. As noted by Baldini, a clock with a similar dial occurs in the fresco of St. Augustine by Botticelli in the Ognissanti. Beneath the blue ground in the central section, to which the later of the two documents refers, is a green ground surrounded by a painted moulding. It is suggested by Baldini, that the gilded star, which is also mentioned in the document, may have been of the same form as the star in the contemporary window of 'The Nativity.' The four male heads in the corners of the rectangle are described by Crowe and Cavalcaselle (*A History of Painting in Italy*, iv, 1911, p. 114n.) as 'so damaged that they give no clue to the master's style'. This erroneous impression is corrected by Poggi (loc. cit). and Boeck (loc. cit.), who notes that the condition of the two upper heads is superior to that of the two heads below. The right half of the head in the lower left corner is the most seriously impaired. In all four heads the removal of repaint during the recent cleaning has resulted in stronger definition and greater legibility. The iconography of the heads is uncertain, and there is no documentary

III. RECONSTRUCTION OF THE CLOCK-FACE
IN THE DUOMO, FLORENCE (*after cleaning*)

justification for assuming that prophets are portrayed. Fahy (verbally) notes that derivatives from the four heads of Prophets occur on a painted frame surrounding a circular stucco relief in the Staatliche Museen, Berlin-Dahlem. The frame is correctly given by Weisbach ('Der Meister des Carrandschen Triptychons,' in *Jarhbuch der Königlich Preuszischen Kunstsammlungen*, xxii, 1901, p. 40) and Giovannozzi ('Note su Giovanni di Francesco,' in *Rivista d'Arte*, vi, 1934, p. 345) to Giovanni di Francesco.

THE NATIVITY and THE RESURRECTION
Duomo, Florence.

PLATES 29–30

Stained glass. Diameter: 473 cm. and 468 cm. respectively.

The construction of the eight circular windows in the cupola of Sta Maria del Fiore was completed in 1431 (Poggi, *Il Duomo di Firenze*, 1909, p. lxxxvii). In 1433 three of the windows were blocked with canvas, and a project was advanced for filling one of them with glass. Cartoons for this window, which was to contain a 'Coronation of the Virgin', were submitted in December 1433 by Ghiberti, and in April of the following year by Donatello, whose cartoon was preferred. The window of 'The Coronation of the Virgin' was completed from Donatello's design by the glass-painters Domenico di Piero da Pisa and Angelo di Lippo in 1438. In July 1443, Ghiberti received a payment for the cartoon for a window of 'The Ascension', which was executed by the glass-painter Bernardo di Francesco in 1444. A payment to Uccello of 2 May 1443, for a cartoon of

'The Ascension' (Poggi, op. cit., p. 143) seems to imply that in the case of this as of the preceding window two alternative cartoons were prepared. At the same time or shortly afterwards, cartoons for two further windows, with 'The Agony in the Garden' and 'The Presentation in the Temple', were prepared by Ghiberti, and in February 1444, Andrea del Castagno received a payment for the cartoon of 'The Deposition'. On 21 February 1443, Uccello's name appears as one of two witnesses to the commissioning of two windows for the cupola from the glass-painter Carlo di Francesco Zati, and on the following day Uccello was entrusted with the designs of two windows to be completed in the course of March of the same year. The subjects of these windows are elucidated by payments to Uccello on 8 July 1443 for a cartoon of 'The Resurrection', and on 5 November 1443 for a cartoon of 'The Nativity'. On 18 February 1444, Uccello received a further payment for a cartoon of 'The Annunciation'. The execution of the windows of 'The Resurrection' and 'The Nativity' was entrusted respectively to Bernardo di Francesco and Angelo di Lippo. Bernardo di Francesco was also responsible for executing the window of 'The Annunciation', which was destroyed in 1828. A further payment to Uccello on 28 January 1445, 'pro ristoro et additione quod fit sibi pro suo labore picture duorum oculaorum' does not refer, as suggested by Van Straelen (*Studien zur Florentiner Glasgemälde*, 1938, p. 86), to restoration of the windows, but to the repair of the cartoons. The two windows are studied in detail by Van Straelen (op. cit., pp. 86–8), who concludes that in both cases the drawing on the window is the work of the glass-painter and not of Uccello and by Marchini (*Le Vetrate Italiane*, 1956, pp. 42, 230). In the 'Resurrection' the body of Christ is made up. The two windows were restored prior to 1954 when they were shown in the *Mostra di quattro maestri del primo rinascimento* (Palazzo Strozzi, Florence, Nos. 8, 9).

The statement of Milanesi (Vasari, *Vite*, ed. Milanesi, ii, 1906, p. 211n.) that in 1434 Uccello prepared a cartoon for a circular window in the Cappella di San Zenobio in the Duomo is refuted by Van Straelen (loc. cit.). The references of Boeck ('Uccello-Studien', in *Zeitschrift für Kunstgeschichte*, ii, 1933, pp. 250–74, and *Paolo Uccello*, 1939, pp. 3, 98) to this presumed commission are incorrect.

THE FLOOD and THE RECESSION OF THE FLOOD: THE SACRIFICE OF NOAH and THE DRUNKENNESS OF NOAH

PLATES 31–48

Chiostro Verde, Sta Maria Novella, Florence.

Fresco (transferred). Upper scene 215 × 510 cm. Lower scene 277 × 540 cm.

For early literature see note to Plates 1–2 above. The statement of Vasari (*Vite*, ed. Milanesi, ii, 1906, p. 153) that Dello Delli 'fu ritratto in Santa Maria Novella da Paolo Uccelli, di chiaroscuro, nella storia, dove Noe è inebriato da Cam suo figliuolo' has given rise to the

IV. G. ROSSI: ENGRAVING AFTER UCCELLO'S 'FLOOD'

V. ENGRAVING AFTER UCCELLO'S 'SACRIFICE OF NOAH'

now widely accepted hypothesis that the frescoes were painted in 1446–8, when Dello Delli, who had left for Spain in 1432 returned to Florence. The historical validity of Vasari's statement is too uncertain for much weight to attach to this argument. An earlier dating is proposed by Berenson (*Italian Pictures of the Renaissance*, 1932, p. 582), and a later dating 'fra il '55 e il '60' by Longhi ('Fatti di Masolino e di Masaccio', in *La Critica d'Arte*, xxv–vi, 1940, p. 179). Though Berenson (*Italian Pictures of the Renaissance: Florentine School*, 1963, p. 209, and earlier editions) groups the two frescoes with the Genesis scenes in the cloister as early works of Uccello, and though Procacci (*Sinopie e affreschi*, 1960, pp. 64 f.) on the evidence of the *sinopie* regards the Genesis scenes as mature works executed at the same time as 'The Flood', the possibility that the two frescoes were executed concurrently with or immediately after the earlier bay in the Chiostro Verde can be ruled out. Within Uccello's work a *terminus post quem* for the scenes is supplied by the complex of works in the Duomo of 1443–4. Of decisive importance for the dating of the scenes is their relevance to the style of Donatello's roundels in the Old Sacristy and of his Paduan reliefs, and especially to 'The Miracle of the Penitent Son', in which a scheme somewhat similar to that of the lunette is employed. It is presumed by Salmi (*Paolo Uccello, Andrea del Castagno, Domenico Veneziano*, 1938, p. 147) that Donatello's relief, which dates from 1447 (not 1449), is based on Uccello's lunette. If, as is more probable, Uccello's lunette was influenced by Donatello's relief, this may well have been executed about 1450–1455.

The iconography of the upper scene, which is most clearly seen in the engraving by G. Rossi reproduced in Rosini's *Storia della pittura italiana*, Pisa, 1839, pl. vol. 1, pl. xxx (Fig. iv), is described by Vasari (ed. cit., pp. 209–10) in a passage which serves to elucidate the dramatic intention in parts of the now abraded fresco: 'ed in essa con tanta fatica e con tant'arte e diligenza lavoro i morti, la tempesta, il furore de' venti, i lampi delle saette, il troncare degli alberi, e la paura degli uomini, che piu non si puo dire. Ed in iscorto fece in prospettiva un morto, al quale un corbo gli cava gli occhi, ed un putto annegato; che per aver il corpo pieno d'acqua fa di quello un arco grandissimo. Dimostrovvi ancora varj effetti umani: come il poco timore dell'acqua in due che a cavallo combattono, e l'estrema paura del morire in una femmina e in un maschio che sono a cavallo in su una bufola, la quale, per le parti di dreto empiendosi d'acqua, fa disperare in tutto coloro di poter salvarsi: opera tuta di tanta bonta ed eccellenza, che gli acquisto grandissima fama'. The details of the crow pecking out the eyes of a dead man, and the body of a drowned youth represented as an arc, noted by Vasari, occur on the extreme right of the lunette; the two fighting figures are those in the left foreground; and the woman stricken with terror is presumably the seated figure in the centre of the scene. Other details not mentioned by Vasari and now more clearly visible in an engraving of the fresco than in the lunette itself, are a figure on the left endeavouring

to secure a foothold on the lower edge of the ark, a kneeling figure further back emerging from the water, a standing man beside him on a raft endeavouring to beat off with his club a bear in the water beside him, a man in the centre floating in a tub, and a male figure immersed in water clasping the ankles of a man standing on a small island of dry land on the right. Clark (*Leon Battista Alberti on Painting*, 1944, p. 18) connects the presence of a wind-god in the right centre of the upper part of the fresco with Alberti's injunction in the *Della Pittura* (*Leone Battista Alberti's kleinere Kunsttheoretische Schriften*, ed. Janitschek, 1877, p. 131) that 'stara bene in la pictura porvi la faccia del vento Zeffiro o Austro che soffi fra le nuvole onde i panni ventoleggino'. A naked figure in the centre background with back turned is copied from the so-called *Gnudo della Paura*, a bronze statuette based on the antique of which versions were in the Medici collection and which was also imitated by Gozzoli and other artists. There is some doubt as to the identity of the standing figure in the right foreground, who is identified by Salmi (op. cit., p. 31) as Noah; since Noah is also represented as a bearded figure at a window of the ark, a type consistent with that employed in the left half of the lower scene, this interpretation is unacceptable. It must be stressed that the lunette represents not one scene, as supposed by Boeck (*Paolo Uccello*, 1939, p. 113), but two, on the left 'The Flood' and on the right 'The Recession of the Flood'. In the left-hand scene we look along the side of the ark and in the right-hand scene across the end. It is not impossible that in the two bodies an attempt is made to reproduce the relationship of one to six presumed by the figures of fifty and three hundred cubits respectively for the breadth and length of the ark in Genesis. White (*The Birth and Rebirth of Pictorial Space*, 1957, pp. 204 f.) observes that the wooden structures to right and left vanish to separate points and concludes from this that Uccello makes use of a Euclidean not an Albertian system of projection. There can, however, be little doubt that the intention was to produce the optical illusion of two converging structures, and that the method of projection is an extension or elaboration of the method advocated by Alberti. An analysis of the space structure by Gioseffi ('Complementi di prospettiva, 2: di Apollodoro d'Atene, di Filippo, di Paolo e d'altre cose,' in *Critica d'Arte*, v, 1958, pp. 123, 134, 135) is fanciful.

The left-hand scene below, engraved for Seroux d'Agincourt, *Histoire de l'Art par les Monuments*, 1823, vi, Pl. 146 (Fig. v), shows 'The Sacrifice of Noah' (Genesis viii. 20) with seven figures and Noah ('the eighth person,' 2 Peter ii. 5) grouped round an altar. Above is a foreshortened figure of God the Father and a rainbow (Genesis x. 13), and on the left a now obliterated unicorn, horse, bull, cow and kids, with birds flying above them. The pyramidal ark, shown in the background of 'The Sacrifice of Noah', recurs on Ghiberti's Gate of Paradise; it is explained by D. C. Allen (*The Legend of Noah*, 1949, p. 169) and Wind ('The Revival of Origen', in *Studies in Art and Literature*

Catalogue

for Belle da Costa Greene, 1954, pp. 412–24) as an allusion to Origen's *In Genesim Homiliae*, ii. In the right-hand scene, Ham stands beneath a vine-covered trellis in right profile, gazing into a hut or penthouse in which Shem and Japhet, with averted heads, stand above the now obliterated figure of Noah. An analysis by Campani ('Uccello's Story of Noah in the Chiostro Verde', in *The Burlington Magazine*, xvii, 1910, pp. 203–10) of the cartoon discovered beneath the right-hand scene when the upper and lower frescoes were removed from the wall in 1909 shows that the wall was originally covered with whitewash on which (as in the case of the earlier scenes) a cartoon was drawn, and that this cartoon was again whitewashed and a further variant prepared. The outstanding difference between the cartoon and the fresco is that the rear figure (?Shem) is shown turned to the left towards Ham and not in full face as in the fresco. Campani notes that the pose of Noah shown in the engraving of Calendi (Fig. VI) after this part of the fresco (*L'Etruria Pittrice*, i, 1791, No. XIV) is incorrect. The *sinopie* found under the two

VI. CALENDI: ENGRAVING AFTER UCCELLO'S 'DRUNKENNESS OF NOAH'

frescoes were destroyed in 1909 (for this see Procacci, *Sinopie e affreschi*, 1960, p. 40, fig. liii, liv). Their significance is discussed by Borsook (*The Mural Painters of Tuscany*, 1960, pp. 147 ff.), who shows that Uccello made three different outlines for the naked youth in left profile in the left centre foreground of 'The Flood'. It is no longer possible to reconstruct the overall colouristic effect of the lower scene, but with its dark blue ground, rainbow, and brown trellis decorated with the green leaves of the vine, this may well have been somewhat stronger than in the earlier bay. The two frescoes were cleaned prior to 1957, when they were shown at the *Mostra di affreschi staccati* (Forte di Belvedere, Florence, Nos. 65, 66), and much new detail was revealed at this time.

PORTRAIT OF A YOUNG MAN
Musée Benoit-Molin, Chambéry.
PLATE 49

Panel: 47 × 36 cm.

Prior to 1956, when it was included in the exhibition *De Giotto à Bellini: Les primitifs italiens dans les musées*

VII. FLORENTINE SCHOOL: PORTRAIT OF A YOUNG MAN. *National Gallery of Art, Washington (Mellon collection)*

de France, the portrait suffered from local retouching and some areas of repaint, and the judgements formed on it before this time were in consequence provisional. Pudelko ('The Early Works of Paolo Uccello', in *The Art Bulletin*, xvi, 1934, p. 249n.) suggests that the original form of the turban was wider. The incised inscription on the parapet EL.FIN. FATVTTO. is unique in Italian portraits of this date, and perhaps derives from a Flemish model (e.g. the male portrait by Jan van Eyck of 1432 with the inscription LEAL. SOVVENIR in the National Gallery, London). Lipman ('The Florentine Profile Portrait', in *The Art Bulletin*, xviii, 1936, p. 101) states that the inscription was 'added later'; this explanation is correct in so far as X-ray photographs (for which see Hatfield, 'Five Early Renaissance Portraits', in *The Art Bulletin*, xlvii, 1965, p. 327n.) show that the ledge is painted over the sitter's coat. Neither technically nor epigraphically is there any reason to suppose that this part of the painting does not date from the middle of the fifteenth century. Pudelko (loc. cit.) regards the feature as 'an independent creation of both painters'. The attribution to Uccello is due to Longhi ('Un ritratto di Paolo Uccello', in *Vita Artistica*, ii, 1927, p. 45; and *Piero della Francesca*, 1947, p. 89), and is accepted by Pudelko (loc. cit.; and 'Florentiner Porträts der Frührenaissance', in *Pantheon*, 1935, pp. 94–5), Salmi (*Paolo Uccello, Andrea del Castagno, Domenico Veneziano*, 1938, p. 144 as ?Uccello), L. Venturi ('Paolo Uccello', in *L'Arte*, xxxiii, 1930, p. 63), Van Marle (*The Development of the Italian Schools of Painting*, x, 1928, p. 240), Micheletti (*Mostra di quattro maestri del primo rinascimento*, Florence, 1954, No. 7),

VIII. DOMENICO VENEZIANO (?): MATTEO OLIVIERI
National Gallery of Art, Washington (Mellon collection)

IX. DOMENICO VENEZIANO (?): MICHELE OLIVIERI
John D. Rockefeller collection, New York

Laclotte (*De Giotto à Bellini: Les primitifs italiens dans les musées de France*, Paris, 1956, No. 122, pp. 90 f.) Sindona (*Paolo Uccello*, 1957, p. 61) and Berti ('Una nuova Madonna e degli appunti su un grande maestro', in *Pantheon*, xix, 1961, p. 304). The attribution to Uccello is rejected by Berenson (*Italian Pictures of the Renaissance*, 1932, p. 335, as ?Masaccio), Lipman (loc. cit., as Follower of Masaccio), Boeck (*Paolo Uccello*, 1939, p. 120, no alternative attribution), Meiss ('Primitifs italiens à l'Orangerie', in *La Revue des Arts*, vi, 1956, p. 141, as a fifteenth-century copy perhaps from a work by Masaccio), Carli (*Tutta la pittura di Paolo Uccello*, 2nd ed., 1959, pp. 28–9, 61, as style of Domenico Veneziano), Hatfield (op. cit., pp. 329 f., as Tuscan, mid-fifteenth century, perhaps by Domenico di Bartolo) and Pope-Hennessy (*The Portrait in the Renaissance*, 1966, pp. 35–6, 307n.). A dating about 1430–5 proposed by Lipman (op. cit., p. 64) is acceptable. The meaning of the inscription has not been explained; its significance is likely to be commemorative.

Boeck (loc. cit.) wrongly links the Chambéry portrait with a 'Portrait of a Young Man' in the National Gallery of Art, Washington (Fig. VII), which was first brought into relation with Uccello by Schmarsow (*Masaccio-Studien*, v, 1900, Pl. viii(a)), on the basis of a reproduction in the catalogue of the Artaud de Montor collection (*Collection de tableaux rapportée*

d'Italie et publiée par M. le Chevalier Artaud de Montor, 1843, No. 115, Pl. 48), where the panel was ascribed to Masaccio. The ascription to Masaccio is maintained by Berenson and Salmi (*Masaccio*, 1947, pp. 174–5), and in the catalogue of the National Gallery of Art (*Preliminary Catalogue of Paintings and Sculpture*, 1941, p. 125). An attribution to a follower of Paolo Uccello is advanced by Lipman (op. cit., p. 101). Boeck (loc. cit.) notes correctly that the style of the Washington and Chambéry portraits is inconsistent with that of the profile portraits of Matteo and Michele Olivieri in the National Gallery of Art, Washington, and the John D. Rockefeller collection, New York (Figs. VIII, IX), which, in common with L. Venturi (op. cit., pp. 63–4; and *Pitture italiane in America*, 1931, Pl. clxiv), Pudelko ('The Early Works of Paolo Uccello', in *The Art Bulletin*, xvi, 1934, pp. 249–50), and Mrs. Kennedy (*Alesso Baldovinetti*, 1938, p. 132), he attributes to Uccello. There is a significant lack of unanimity in the dating proposed for the Olivieri portraits by those critics who ascribe them to Uccello, Boeck favouring a dating about 1425, Pudelko associating them with the earlier and Venturi with the later Chiostro Verde frescoes, and Mrs. Kennedy regarding them as late works. Both portraits are given to Uccello by Sindona (*Paolo Uccello*, 1957, p. 30) with a dating ca. 1433–4. For these panels the attribution of Berenson (*Italian Pictures of the Renaissance*, 1932, p. 172) and Salmi (op.

149

Catalogue

X. BALDOVINETTI: PORTRAIT OF A LADY.
National Gallery, London

XI. THE MASTER OF THE CASTELLO 'NATIVITY':
PORTRAIT OF A LADY. *Lehman collection, New York*

XII. FLORENTINE SCHOOL: PORTRAIT OF A LADY.
Metropolitan Museum, New York (Bache collection)

XIII. FLORENTINE SCHOOL: PORTRAIT OF A LADY.
Gardner Museum, Boston

XIV. FLORENTINE SCHOOL: PORTRAIT OF A LADY.
National Gallery of Victoria, Melbourne

cit., p. 173) to Domenico Veneziano, and a dating shortly before 1440 are to be preferred.

None of the female portraits with which he has been credited has any reasonable claim to be considered as Uccello's. The 'Portrait of a Lady' in the National Gallery, No. 758 (Fig. x), ascribed to Uccello by Morelli, Richter (*Italian Art in the National Gallery*, 1883, p. 17), Loeser ('Paolo Uccello', in *Repertorium für Kunstwissenschaft*, xii, 1898, p. 88), Van Marle (*The Development of the Italian Schools of Painting*, x, 1928, p. 236), Boeck (op. cit., p. 114) and Longhi ('Il "Maestro di Pratovecchio"', in *Paragone*, iii, 1952, No. 35, p. 32n.) is by Baldovinetti (for decisive arguments in favour of this attribution see Fry, 'A Profile Portrait by Baldovinetti', in *The Burlington Magazine*, xviii, 1911, p. 311; Kennedy, *Alesso Baldovinetti*, 1938, pp. 131–3; and Davies, *National Gallery Catalogues: The Earlier Italian Schools*, 1961, pp. 42–3). Three female portraits in the Lehman collection, New York (Fig. xi), the Metropolitan Museum, New York (Bache Collection) (Fig. XII) and the Gardner Museum, Boston (Fig. XIII) have also been given to Uccello. The attribution to Uccello of the Lehman portrait is endorsed by L. Venturi ('Paolo Uccello', in *L'Arte*, xxxiii, 1930, p. 64; *Pitture italiane in America*, 1931, pl. clxi), Sindona (*Paolo Uccello*, 1957, p. 41, as a late autograph work) and Berti ('Una nuova Madonna e degli

appunti su un grande maestro', in *Pantheon*, xix, 1961, p. 304). The Bache portrait is ascribed to Uccello by L. Venturi (loc. cit.), Salmi (op. cit., pp. 25, 142), Micheletti (*Mostra di quattro maestri del primo rinascimento*, 1954, No. 17, as attributed to Uccello), Sindona (*Paolo Uccello*, 1957, p. 40), Carli (*Tutta la pittura di Paolo Uccello*, 2nd. ed., 1959, pp. 30–1, 55–6), and Berti (loc. cit.). Uccello's authorship of the Gardner portrait is sustained by L. Venturi (loc. cit.), Van Marle (op. cit., p. 236), and Berti (loc. cit.). Offner ('La Mostra del Tesoro di Firenze Sacra', in *Burlington Magazine*, lxiii, 1933, p. 178) and Lipman ('Three Profile Portraits by the Master of the Castello "Nativity"', in *Art in America*, 1936, pp. 11–24, and 'The Florentine Profile Portrait', in *Art Bulletin*, xviii, 1936, p. 72) give all three female portraits to the Master of the Castello Nativity. This attribution is contested, and that of the Bache portrait to Uccello is sustained, by Salmi ('La Madonna dantesca del museo di Livorno e il Maestro della Natività di Castello', in *Liburni Civitas*, xi, 1938, pp. 38–40, 44). Berenson (*Italian Pictures of the Renaissance: Florentine School*, 1963, p. 142) attributes the Lehman portrait to the Master of the Castello Nativity, and associates the Bache and Gardner portraits (op. cit., p. 62) with Domenico Veneziano. The ascription to the Master of the Castello Nativity is accepted in the first edition of this book for all three paintings, but is in practice applicable only to the Lehman portrait. The Bache and Gardner portraits appear to have been painted by a single hand, which is wrongly identified by Pudelko ('Florentiner Porträts der Frührenaissance' in *Pantheon*, 1935, p. 95) as that of the Master of the Karlsruhe 'Adoration'. Other female portraits wrongly ascribed to Uccello are in the Johnson collection, Philadelphia, No. 34 (Perkins, 'Pitture italiane nella raccolta Johnson a Filadelfia', in *Rassegna d'Arte*, v, 1905, p. 115), for which Mrs. Kennedy (op. cit., p. 131) suggests a plausible attribution to Neri di Bicci, and in the National Museum, Melbourne (ex-Cook collection; Van Marle, op. cit., p. 236, as ?Uccello) (Fig. XIV). The latter panel is Lippesque.

MALE HEAD IN LEFT PROFILE
Uffizi, Florence (Gabinetto dei Disegni, No. 28E).
PLATE 50

Bistre wash on white paper, background coloured dark brown. 29 × 20 cm.

Berenson (*The Drawings of the Florentine Painters*, 1938, No. 2766, i, p. 15) as Uccello. Berenson's classic appreciation reads: 'Relieved against a dark brown surface, washed in with bistre on a white ground, we see the profile of an iron-tempered master of life. It has not been easy for him to win the prize away from his rivals, and in the struggle his forehead has over-beetled his face, and his underlip has curled down as if to meet his chin; but he has remained master—and with the loss of such a trifle as a name, master he still is. Types so life-enhancing by the vigour of their being are not at any time offered in plenty either by life or art.

Catalogue

He was lucky to find Uccello to portray him. You may wander through all the precincts of Renaissance painting without finding a portrait superior to this profile in the qualities that are essential to a masterpiece.' The ascription of the sheet to Uccello is accepted by Salmi (*Paolo Uccello, Andrea del Castagno, Domenico Veneziano*, 1938, pp. 152–4), Boeck (*Paolo Uccello*, 1939, p. 127) and most other critics. Beenken ('Zum Werke des Masaccio, I', in *Zeitschrift für Bildende Kunst*, lxiii, 1929, p. 119) attributes the drawing to Masaccio, Hartt ('A new Attribution for a famous Drawing', in *Art Quarterly*, xix, 1956, pp. 162–73) gives it to Castagno, and Stix and Fröhlich-Bum (*Albertina-Katalog*, iii, 1932, No. 12) reject the attribution to Uccello. A resemblance to Castagno's Niccolò da Tolentino fresco is noted by Horster ('Castagnos Florentiner Fresken 1450–1457', in *Wallraf-Richartz Jahrbuch*, xvii, 1955, p. 113), who concurs in the traditional ascription to Uccello. Reasonably close analogies for the handling of the features are to be found in the later Chiostro Verde frescoes. Hartt (loc. cit.) reproduces three photographs, made about 1910 and in 1930 and 1954, which illustrate the progressive deterioration of the sheet.

THE ROUT OF SAN ROMANO

(*i*) *National Gallery, London, No. 583;* (*ii*) *Uffizi, Florence, No. 52 (479);* (*iii*) *Louvre, Paris, No. 1273.*
PLATES 51–76; Frontispiece

Panel: (i) 182×319 cm., (ii) 182×322 cm., (iii) 180×316 cm.

The three panels are first mentioned in 1492 in an inventory of the property of Lorenzo de' Medici (Florence, Archivio di Stato, Archivio mediceo inanzi il principato, transcribed by Horne, 'The Battle-piece by Uccello in the National Gallery', in *The Monthly Review*, v, 1901, p. 137): 'Nella chamera grande terrena, detta Lachamera di Lorenzo . . . Sej quadri chorniciatj atorno & messj dor.° sopra ladetta spalliera et sopra allettuccio dj braccia 42 lunghi et altj braccia iij½ dipintj Cioe tre della rotta di san Romano & uno dj battaglie & (?dj) draghj et lionj et vno della storia diparis di mano di pagholo vcello & vno dimano difranc° dipesello entrovj vna caccia. Fiorinj 300.' They are listed again in an inventory of the contents of the Palazzo Medici of 1598 (Florence, Archivio di Stato, Guardaroba No. 198, transcribed by Horne, op. cit., p. 188): '3 quadri grandi di giostre antichi tutti in uno pezzo, con lor corniciette dorate, apicchati almuro alti sopra alla porta del primo salone, nellandito della cappella'. Between these dates the panels are mentioned by the Anonimo Magliabechiano (*Il Codice Magliabechiano*, herausgegeben von Carl Frey, 1892, p. 100: 'Dipinse e quadri delle giostre nel palazo de Medicj nella uia Largha') and in the 1568 edition of the *Vite* of Vasari (*Vite*, ed. Milanesi, ii, 1906, p. 208: 'In casa Medici dipinse in tela a tempera alcuni storie di animali . . . e nell'altre tele fece alcune mostre d'uomini d'arme a cavalli di quei tempi, con assai ritratti di naturale'). The subsequent history of the panels cannot

now be reconstructed; that in the Uffizi reached the gallery between 1769 and 1784, and those in the Louvre and National Gallery appear to have been acquired from the Giraldi family by Lombardi and Baldi between 1844 and 1848 (Milanesi, in Vasari, *Vite*, ed. cit., ii, p. 214n.). One of the two latter panels was subsequently in the Campana collection (*Cataloghi del Museo Campana*, 1859, classe VIII, No. 166), and was purchased in 1861 for the Musée Napoléon III (Reiset, *Notice des tableaux du Musée Napoléon III*, 1863, No. 99, pp. 40–1). The third panel was purchased with the Lombardi-Baldi collection in 1857 for the National Gallery. In early catalogues of the Louvre and the National Gallery and by Milanesi (*Vite*, ed. cit., ii, 1906, pp. 213–14n.) and other writers, the panels are identified with four panels painted by Uccello in the Orto de' Bartolini in Valfonda: 'ed in Gualfonda particolarmente, nell'orto che era de' Bartolini, e, in un terrazzo, di sua mano quattro storie di legname, piene di guerre; crioe cavalli e uomini armati, con portature di que' tempi bellissime: e fra gli uomini e ritratto Paolo Orsino, Ottobuono da Parma, Luca da Canale, e Carlo Malatesti, signor di Rimini; tutti capitani generali di quei tempi. Et i detti quadri furono a' nostri tempi, perche erano guasti ed avevano patito, fatti racconciare da Giuliano Bugiardini, che piuttosto ha loro nociuto che giovato.' It was assumed by Horne (loc. cit.), on the basis of the 1492 inventory, that the three paintings filled one end of the room which in 1492 was used as the bed-chamber of Lorenzo de' Medici, and were divided from one another by pilasters. The room also contained three paintings on canvas, a combat of dragons and lions by Uccello, a scene from the legend of Paris by Uccello, and a chase, probably representing lions fighting among themselves, by Pesellino. Technical examination and cleaning (see below) has, however, shown that the paintings were not originally rectangular, and that the upper corners have been made up (perhaps in the sixteenth century, when the paintings were transferred to the room in which they are recorded in 1598). Baldini ('Restauri di dipinti fiorentini in occasione della mostra di Quattro Maestri del Rinascimento,' in *Bolletino d'Arte*, xxxix, 1954, pp. 221–40) concludes that the form of the upper corners was determined by the corbels of the room for which the paintings were designed, and suggests that the panels in London and Florence were set, from left to right, on the entrance wall of the room, and that the panel in Paris was set at right angles to them. This case is accepted, with reserve, by Davies (*National Gallery Catalogues: the Earlier Italian Schools*, 1961, pp. 525–31), who points out that the three panels are lit uniformly from the left and that the top edges of the panels in London and Florence are cut, possibly in consequence of the removal of an arched section above. There is no reason to question Horne's belief that the paintings in the room were set above the level of the doorways, and that their base would thus have been at least seven feet from the ground.

The Rout of San Romano, which is stated in the inventory of 1492 to form the subject of the paintings, took place on 1 June 1432. Since the preceding April, Florentine territory had been ravaged by Sienese forces under the command of Bernardino della Carda, who had earlier been in Florentine employment and was at that time serving under the Duke of Milan. Following the loss of certain fortresses, Micheletto Attendoli da Cotignola, the Florentine commander, was replaced by Niccolò Maurucci da Tolentino, being retained in a subordinate position with the title of 'Governatore'. At sunrise on 1 June, Niccolò da Tolentino, who had been separated from his main force and was accompanied by not more than twenty horsemen, was surprised by the Sienese forces near the tower of San Romano. After resisting valiantly for eight hours, Niccolò da Tolentino was relieved by Micheletto da Cotignola, whose forces, crossing the Arno, set upon the Sienese rear and clinched the victory. Reading from left to right, the three panels represent: (i) National Gallery, 'Niccolò da Tolentino directing the Attack at San Romano', (ii) Uffizi, 'The Unhorsing of Bernardino della Carda', (iii) Louvre, 'Micheletto da Cotignola leading the Counter-Attack of the Florentine Squadrons'. The identity of the first scene is established by a banner with the device of Niccolò da Tolentino, the 'groppo di Salamone' (Solomon's knot). The third contains the standard of Micheletto da Cotignola (2 and 3, barry undee, argent and sable: 4, gules, an impress of a unicorn sejant or, with a scroll argent). The second scene is stated by Horne (op. cit., p. 130) not to contain any portrait figure, but in view of the prominence given to the horseman in the centre and of the character of the outer scenes, it is likely that the opposing commander is represented. The banners hanging from the trumpets shown in all three scenes are presumed by Horne (op. cit., p. 133) to be emblazoned with the ensigns of the various squadrons of the Florentine force.

The first of the panels to be cleaned was that in the Louvre, which is described by Horne (op. cit., p. 134) as 'in still worse condition than the companion scenes'. As a result of this cleaning the silvering on the armour was revealed. The Uffizi panel (for which see Baldini, loc. cit.) was cleaned prior to 1954. The principal changes were in the upper part of the painting, which had been much overpainted, and where much new detail was revealed. The cleaning of the painting in London produced a generally similar result. As noted by Davies (loc. cit.), it revealed 'a striking increase in refinement, but very little change in the forms'. There was evidence of a pentimento in the head of the youth in right profile at the left. The panels in their cleaned state offer a clearer indication of Uccello's colouristic intentions than they did previously, but their overall condition is unsatisfactory and the loss of surface modelling, as a result of earlier restoration, is very marked.

There is no firm date for the three panels. Horne (op. cit., pp. 120–1) supposes that the panels were begun after 1451, when the construction of the palace was virtually complete, and before 1457, when Pesellino died. They would thus have preceded the decoration of

the chapel by Benozzo Gozzoli (1459) and that of the Sala Grande by Antonio Pollajuolo (1460). Since, however, there is no unity of programme between the scenes on the lateral wall (which were very probably begun by Pesellino before his death and completed by Uccello) and the 'Rout of San Romano' at the end of the same room, the decoration of the two walls may not have been proceeded with concurrently. Apart from Crowe and Cavalcaselle (op. and ed. cit., iv, p. 112), Marangoni ('Una predella di Paolo Uccello' in *Dedalo*, xii, 1931–2, p. 3), who supposes that they were executed after the battle in 1432, and Antal ('Gedanken zur Entwicklung der Trecento- und Quattrocentomalerei in Siena und Florenz', in *Jahrbuch für Kunstwissenschaft*, 1924–5, p. 207; 'Studien zur Gotik im Quattrocento', in *Jahrbuch der Preuszischen Kunstsammlungen*, xlvi, 1925, p. 3), criticism almost unanimously supports a dating in the mid-fifties. In favour of this view are Boeck (*Paolo Uccello*, 1939, pp. 52–62), Longhi ('Fatti di Masolino e di Masaccio', in *La Critica d'Arte*, xxv–vi, 1940, p. 179: 'fra il '55 e il '60'), Pudelko ('The Early Works of Paolo Uccello', in *The Art Bulletin*, xvi, 1934, p. 257: 'in the period 1456–8'), and Salmi (*Paolo Uccello, Andrea del Castagno, Domenico Veneziano*, 1938, p. 39; *Masaccio*, 1947, p. 75: 'intorno al 1456'). Salmi connects the commission with that for Castagno's equestrian figure of Niccolò da Tolentino in the Duomo (1456).

SAINT GEORGE AND THE DRAGON
Musée Jacquemart-André, Paris, No. 1038.
PLATES 77, 79

Panel: 52 × 90 cm.

First discussed by Loeser ('Paolo Uccello', in *Repertorium für Kunstwissenschaft*, xxi, 1898, p. 89) when in the Bardini collection. Bardini sale, London, 1899, 5–7 June, lot 488. Loeser (loc. cit.) proposes a date later than that hypothetically assigned to the Lanckoronski 'St. George and the Dragon'; analogies with a late work, the Urbino predella, are also noted by L. Venturi ('Una risorta casa del rinascimento italiano', in *L'Arte*, xvii, 1914, p. 64) and Van Marle (*Development of the Italian Schools of Painting*, x, 1928, p. 208), who suggests that the panel was executed in Uccello's studio. The panel is placed by Salmi (*Paolo Uccello, Andrea del Castagno, Domenico Veneziano*, 1938, pp. 22–3) and Boeck (*Paolo Uccello*, 1939, p. 110) after the San Miniato frescoes, and is considered by Sindona (*Paolo Uccello*, 1957, p. 27) a youthful work of ca. 1430. A somewhat later dating, ca. 1437–40, is advanced by Carli (*Tutta la pittura di Paolo Uccello*, 2nd ed., 1959, pp. 20, 55). The attribution to Uccello is accepted by Berenson (*Italian Pictures of the Renaissance*, 1932, p. 582; *Italian Pictures of the Renaissance: Florentine School*, 1963, p. 209). Langton Douglas and De Nicola (in Crowe and Cavalcaselle, *A History of Painting in Italy*, iv, 1911, p. 122n.) observe that the handling is 'less forcible' than that of the Oxford 'Hunt', and Pudelko ('The Early Works of Paolo Uccello', in *The Art Bulletin*, xvi, 1934, p. 259n.) gives the panel to the

Catalogue

Master of the Karlsruhe 'Adoration'. Schubring (*Cassoni*, 1915, p. 241) regards the 'St. George' as a work of Uccello's school, and Venturi (*Storia*, vii–i, p. 340) groups it (wrongly) with the Lanckoronski 'St. George', the Berlin tondo of 'The Adoration of the Magi', and the so-called 'Thebaid' in the Accademia at Florence. A decision as to authorship is complicated by the condition of the work, which is much restored. The treatment of the background is related to that of the three panels of 'The Rout of San Romano', and Faison (review of Boeck's *Uccello* in *The Art Bulletin*, xxii, 1940, pp. 282–4) correctly points out that on this account alone Boeck's early dating is unacceptable. The quality of the painting is less high than Fry's appreciation ('Three Pictures in the Jacquemart-André Collection', in *The Burlington Magazine*, xxv, 1914, p. 85) suggests. The dimensions of the panel are consistent with the view that it decorated a *cassone* or chest.

SAINT GEORGE AND THE DRAGON
National Gallery, London, No. 6294.
PLATES 78, 80–2

Canvas: 57 × 73 cm.

Formerly in the collection of Graf Lanckoronski, Vienna.

The attribution to Uccello was first proposed by Loeser ('Paolo Uccello', in *Repertorium für Kunstwissenschaft*, xxi, 1898, pp. 88–9), and is accepted by Van Marle (*Development of the Italian Schools of Painting*, x, 1928, p. 207), Salmi (*Paolo Uccello, Andrea del Castagno, Domenico Veneziano*, 1938, p. 141), Lionello Venturi ('Paolo Uccello', in *L'Arte*, xxxiii, 1930, p. 63), Boeck (*Paolo Uccello*, 1939, p. 116), Pittaluga (*Paolo Uccello* 1946, pp. 13–14), and Berenson (*Italian Pictures of the Renaissance: Florentine School*, 1963, p. 209), who had earlier (*Italian Pictures of the Renaissance*, 1932, p. 342) given it to Giovanni di Francesco. A. Venturi (*Storia*, vii–i, 1911, p. 340) gives the panel, along with the Jacquemart-André 'St. George', to an 'eccellente pittore di cassoni' responsible also for the Berlin 'Adoration of the Magi' (Domenico Veneziano); and Pudelko ('Der Meister der Anbetung in Karlsruhe', in *Das siebente Jahrzehnt: Festschrift zum 70. Geburtstag von Adolph Goldschmidt*, 1935, p. 127) attributes it to the Master of the Karlsruhe 'Adoration'. The quality of the Lanckoronski 'St. George' is appreciably above that of the other works ascribed by Pudelko to this artist. Van Marle proposes a dating before the earlier Chiostro Verde frescoes, and Salmi a dating before the prophets on the clock-face in the Duomo (1443). For reasons argued by Faison (review of Boeck's *Uccello* in *The Art Bulletin*, xxii, 1940, pp. 282–4), the late dating proposed by Boeck (loc. cit.) is more convincing. The painting is dated by Carli (*Tutta la pittura di Paolo Uccello*, 2nd. ed., 1959, pp. 31–2) ca. 1456, and by Sindona ('Elementi critici e fantastici nell'arte di Paolo Uccello', in *L'Arte*, lviii, 1959, pp. 293–7) ca. 1455–60. Davies ('Uccello's St. George in London', in *The Burlington Magazine*, ci, 1959, pp. 308–15; *National Gallery Catalogues: the Earlier Italian Schools*, 1961,

pp. 532–3) accepts the painting as a work by Uccello, and dates it, on grounds of costume, ca. 1460. The fact that the painting is on canvas (like the lost decorations of Uccello and Antonio Pollajuolo for the Palazzo Medici) acts in favour of a dating after about 1455. It is described by Schubring (*Cassoni*, 1915, p. 240), who accepts the ascription to Uccello, as a 'Cornicebild'. Boeck (op. cit., p. 68) notes that the drawing of the horse may have been influenced by that of Castagno's 'Niccolò da Tolentino' (1456). The painting was cleaned after its acquisition by the National Gallery (for this see Brommelle, 'St. George and the Dragon, painting cleaned at the National Gallery', in *Museums Journal*, 1959, pp. 87–95).

THE NATIVITY and ANNUNCIATION TO THE SHEPHERDS
Soprintendenza alle Gallerie, Florence (from San Martino alla Scala).
PLATES 83–4

Fresco (transferred): 140 × 215 cm.

Identified and published by Paatz ('Una Natività di Paolo Uccello e alcune considerazioni sull'arte del Maestro', in *Rivista d'Arte*, xvi, 1934, pp. 111–48). The fresco, which is much damaged, shows the Virgin in the centre turned to the right, kneeling above the Child, St. Joseph seated in left profile in the extreme right foreground, and within the receding perspective of the stable the standing ox and ass; in the left foreground is a seated goat, and behind it in the receding landscape the three seated shepherds and a flock of sheep. As in the Chiostro Verde frecoes, the *terra verde* which determines the tonality of the fresco, is modified by local colouring; the ox and the tree trunks supporting the stable are brown, the interior of the stable roof reddish brown, and the sheep yellow or white, while the strip of decoration framing the fresco is dark green or black. The lunette, which is now in the Deposito degli Uffizi, occupied a bay in the cloister of the former Spedale di San Martino (since 1863 a Casa di Patronato per Minorenni), where it was set over a door leading to the church (for this see Paatz, *Die Kirchen von Florenz*, v, 1952, pp. 142, 146). The history of the hospital throws no light on the date of the fresco, and this is presumed by Paatz to have been executed along with the later frescoes in the Chiostro Verde about 1446. This dating is accepted by Salmi (*Paolo Uccello, Andrea del Castagno, Domenico Veneziano*, 1938, p. 147) and Boeck (*Paolo Uccello*, 1939, p. 114), the former regarding the fresco as a studio work based on a design by the master. In the better-preserved parts there is nothing inconsistent with the view that the fresco was painted by Uccello. It is rightly regarded as an autograph Uccello by Procacci (*Mostra di affreschi staccati*, 1957, p. 56). It is probable that the composition, which is more advanced than that of the 'Flood', belongs in the sixth rather than the fifth decade of the century. Since Uccello's 'Nativity' forms the point of departure for the fresco of the same subject painted by Baldovinetti in 1460–2 in the cloister of the Annunziata, the lunette

XV. OUTLINE DRAWING AFTER UCCELLO'S 'NATIVITY' AT SAN MARTINO ALLA SCALA (*after Paatz*)

must have been completed before this time. The outline reproduction of the fresco included in Paatz's article and illustrated in this book (Fig. xv) is incorrect in that in the fresco the main transversals on the right and left sides coincide. The underlying *sinopia* was uncovered in 1952, was again covered with whitewash, and was removed from the wall only in 1958. It was exhibited, with the fresco, at the *Mostra di affreschi staccati* (1966), and is discussed by Procacci (*Sinopie e affreschi*, 1960, p. 233). The grid of lines in the *sinopia* corresponds exactly with the incised lines of the fresco. White (*The Birth and Rebirth of Pictorial Space*, 1957, p. 205) observes that 'it is as if the adjacent halves of two entire Albertian constructions lying side by side had been incorporated in a single composition'. The *sinopia* is also discussed by Gioseffi ('Complementi di prospettiva, 2: di Apollodoro d'Atene, di Filippo, di Paolo e d'altre cose', in *Critica d'Arte*, v, 1958, pp. 105–6, 110) and Klein ('Pomponius Gauricus on Perspective', in *The Art Bulletin*, xliii, 1961, pp. 211–30). Gioseffi regards the *sinopia* as 'una esatissima, rigorosissima, limpidissima costruzione con punti di distanza', and characterizes the central vertical as an Albertian device, while Klein, stressing the significance of the two distance points in the margins of the *sinopia*, concludes that Uccello 'took upon himself the task of extending the bifocal system to represent a unified space'. A closely analogous perspective scheme is utilized in the first and second scenes of the predella at Urbino.

With regard to the method of construction, it may be noted (i) that the distance between the supports of the stable and the edge of the lunette is equal to half the distance between the two supports; (ii) that the left support of the stable served as the controlling vertical for the perspective construction on the left of the fresco; and (iii) that the distance point for this construction falls in the centre of the fresco. In effect, therefore, a double *costruzione legittima* is employed, linked by the figure of the Virgin kneeling at the point of juncture of the two schemes in the centre foreground of the scene.

PERSPECTIVE STUDY OF A MAZZOCCHIO

Uffizi, Florence (*Gabinetto dei Disegni, No. 1756A*).

Pen on white paper: 9 × 24 cm.

Berenson (*The Drawings of the Florentine Painters*, 1938, No. 2770).

PERSPECTIVE STUDY OF A MAZZOCCHIO

Uffizi, Florence (*Gabinetto dei Disegni, No. 1757A*),

Pen on white paper: 9 × 27 cm.

Berenson (*The Drawings of the Florentine Painters*, 1938, No. 2771).

PERSPECTIVE STUDY OF A CHALICE OR CUP

Uffizi, Florence (*Gabinetto dei Disegni, No. 1758A*).

Pen on white paper: 29 × 24·5 cm.

Berenson (*The Drawings of the Florentine Painters*, 1938, No. 2678).

PLATES 85–6

Vasari (*Vite*, ed. Milanesi, 1906, ii, p. 205) states that Uccello produced 'mazzocchi a punte a quadro tirati in prospettiva per diverse vedute, e palle a settantadue facce a punte di diamanti, e in ogni faccia brucioli avvolti su per i bastoni, e altre bizzarrie', and claims to have included in his *Libro de' Disegni* 'un mazzocchio tirato con linee sole tanto bello, che altro che la pacienza di Paulo non le avrebbe condotto'. The present studies are accepted by Berenson, Salmi, Boeck and most other critics as the sole surviving examples of the class of drawing Vasari had in mind. Boeck (*Paolo Uccello*, 1939, p. 77) regards No. 1758A as a study for the chalice in Uccello's projected altar-piece of the *Institution of the Eucharist*. Parronchi ('Paolo o Piero?', in *Studi su la dolce prospettiva*, Milan, 1964, pp. 533–48) ascribes it to Piero della Francesca on the strength of a passage in Vasari's life of Piero (*Vite*, ed. Milanesi, 1906, ii, p. 491) describing 'un vaso in modo tirato a quadri e facce, che si vede dinanzi, di dietro e dagli lati, il fondo e la bocca'. This attribution, and an attempt to distinguish between the handling of No. 1758A and the two related drawings are alike improbable. The three drawings are analysed by Kern ('Der Mazzocchio des Paolo Uccello' in *Jahrbuch der Preuszischen Kunstsammlungen*, xxxvi, 1915, pp. 13–38). The *mazzocchio*, a wooden or wicker headdress which supported the *foggia* and *becchetto*, was a common article of male attire in Florence in the second and third quarters of the fifteenth century; painted representations of the *mazzocchio* are introduced by Uccello into 'The Flood' and the Louvre panel of 'The Rout of San Romano'. By virtue of its form, which can be clearly determined in these paintings, its representation presented a constructional problem of special complexity, with which later perspective theorists also concerned themselves.

The elaborate system of projection, which can be

Catalogue

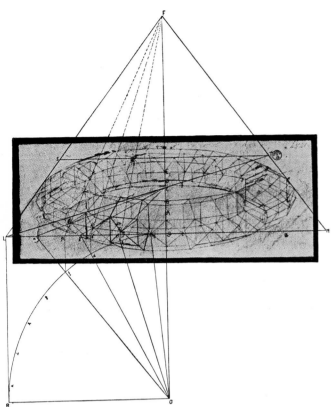

XVI. THE CONSTRUCTION OF UCCELLO'S
MAZZOCCHIO (*after Kern*)

reconstructed from the incised lines on the present sheets, and the relevance of the methods used to the principles of the *costruzione legittima* are discussed by Kern (Fig. XVI). Two sheets in the Louvre (Cabinet des Dessins, Nos. 1969, 1970), showing respectively a sphere and a mazzocchio, are closely related to the three sheets in Florence. When in the possession of Baldinucci, they were ascribed to Uccello, and are given tentatively to Uccello by Bacou and Bean (Rome, Gabinetto Nazionale delle Stampe: *Disegni fiorentini del Museo del Louvre dalla collezione di Filippo Baldinucci*, 1959, Nos. 3, 4).

THE PROFANATION OF THE HOST
Galleria Nazionale delle Marche, Urbino.
PLATES 87–100

Panel: 42 × 351 cm.

Transferred to the Palazzo Ducale in 1861 from the Collegio dei R. P. Scolopi adjacent to the church of Sta Agata, where it served as a predella to 'The Institution of the Eucharist' of Justus of Ghent. Both paintings were previously on the high altar of the demolished church of Corpus Domini, and are described in an inventory published by Scatassa ('Chiesa di Corpus Domini in Urbino', in *Repertorium für Kunstwissenschaft*, xxv, 1902, pp. 438–46): 'Il quadro dell'altare maggiore e dei primi che si dipingessero a olio in tavola rappresentante la Cena degli Apostoli, e di mano di Giusto Todesco pittore habitante in Urbino al tempo

del duca Federico Montefeltro, la cui effigie in esso; ed anche dell'istesso e d'altri l'ornamento di legno indorato antico con un base (predella) in cui si vedono alcuni miracoli del SS.mo Sacramento.'

Documents transcribed by Schmarsow (*Melozzo da Forlì*, 1886, pp. 359–60) from the now missing 'Libro B del Corpus Domini' attest the presence of Uccello in Urbino in 1465, when he received a single small payment, between 10 August 1467 and 27 February 1468, and between 10 August 1468 and 31 October of the same year. Apart from a single reference (at the end of August 1467) to the transportation from Florence of 'gesso volterrano e altri colori', these passages refer exclusively to the provisioning of Uccello and of his son, Donato. If, therefore, we were dependent on these entries alone, we should be forced to conclude with Calzini (*Urbino e i suoi Monumenti*, 1897, p. 143) that 'della tavola che Paolo Uccello dipinse nel 1468 per la chiesa di Corpus Domini non si ha più memoria e nemmeno si conosce il soggetto rappresentatovi dal vecchio maestro'. In practice, however, these payments to Uccello are preceded and followed by negotiations with other artists which are almost certainly to be connected with the same commission. Thus we know that prior to Uccello's arrival in Urbino discussions were opened in June 1466 between the Compagnia di Corpus Domini and an anonymous painter from Foligno; that after Uccello's departure, on 8 April 1469, Piero della Francesca visited Urbino at the instance of the Compagnia di Corpus Domini 'a vedere la taula per farla' (Pungileoni, *Elogio storico di Giovanni Santi*, 1822, pp. 17–18); and that in 1473 the altar-piece of 'The Institution of the Eucharist' was commissioned for the church of Corpus Domini from Justus of Ghent. If, as is plausibly supposed by Bombe ('Zur Kommunion der Aposteln von Josse van Gent in Urbino', in *Zeitschrift für Bildende Kunst*, lxv, 1931, p. 70), these documents refer to one commission, we must believe that in 1466 negotiations for the high altar-piece of the church of Corpus Domini were opened with a painter from Foligno; that the contract was then offered to Uccello, who completed the predella of the altar-piece and began work on the upper section; that Uccello's design was regarded as unsatisfactory; that in the year following his departure from Urbino his unfinished painting was shown to Piero della Francesca, who refused to undertake the altar-piece; and that the commission was ultimately awarded in 1473 to Justus of Ghent. In view of the unity of programme between the upper section of the altar-piece, with 'The Institution of the Eucharist', and the lower section, with 'The Profanation of the Host', it is probable that 'The Institution of the Eucharist' was from the first designated as the subject of the altar-piece; and it is suggested by Bombe that beneath the altar-piece of Justus of Ghent may lie the remains of Uccello's cartoon. An iconographical precedent for 'The Institution of the Eucharist' is provided by a fresco from the studio of Fra Angelico at San Marco, Florence. The exact source of the legend illustrated in the predella has not been established; in the catalogue of the Italian exhibition of

1930 (Royal Academy, London), the scenes are referred mistakenly to a profaned pyx. The predella, which is relatively well preserved, was cleaned in 1954, when some overpainting was removed (for this see Baldini, 'Restauri di dipinti fiorentini in occasione della Mostra di Quattro Maestri del Rinascimento', in *Bollettino d'Arte*, xxxix, 1954, pp. 234–7). As noted by Gioseffi ('Complementi di prospettiva, 2: di Apollodoro d'Atene, di Filippo, di Paolo, e d'altre cose', in *Critica d'Arte*, v, 1958, pp. 105, 124–5) the method of construction in the first two scenes is closely analogous to that in the Nativity fresco. White (*The Birth and Rebirth of Pictorial Space*, 1957, p. 203) observes that the incised lines in the priming of second scene relate to three alternative compositional schemes.

A HUNT
Ashmolean Museum, Oxford
PLATES 101–6
Panel: 65×165 cm.
Collection Fox-Strangways (till 1850).

The attribution to Uccello is due to Loeser ('Paolo Uccello', in *Repertorium für Kunstwissenschaft*, xxi, 1898, pp. 87–8), who associated the panel correctly with the Urbino predella and suggested that it was originally part of a *cassone*. It is claimed by Schubring (*Cassoni*, 1915, p. 242) that the titles 'Staghunt in a Forest by Night', 'Caccia Notturna' and 'Nächtliche Jagdszene', by which the panel is often described, are incorrect, and that the scene takes place by day. Since a crescent moon is shown in the sky in the centre of the painting, this contention is inadmissible. In the attribution to Uccello, the only dissentient is A. Venturi (*Storia dell'Arte Italiana*, VII–i, 1911, p. 340), who wrongly connects the panel with the Berlin 'Adoration of the Magi', later recognized as a work of Domenico Veneziano. The 'Hunt' is regarded by Marangoni ('Una predella di Paolo Uccello', in *Dedalo*, xii, 1931–2, p. 3) and Van Marle (*Development of the Italian Schools of Painting*, x, 1928, pp. 209–10) as a work executed before 1436, in the case of the latter on account of the 'charming Gothic line' formed by the hounds. By most other critics it is considered a late work, datable after 1460. Salmi (*Paolo Uccello, Andrea del Castagno, Domenico Veneziano*, 1938, pp. 151–2) refers to a number of hunting poems providing loose literary parallels for the representation, and suggests that the scene may depict the young Lorenzo de' Medici hunting in the *pineta* of Pisa. On account of the dimensions of the panel, Salmi rejects a verbal suggestion of Gronau that the 'Hunt' is perhaps identical with a painting listed in an Urbino inventory (A. S. F. Urbino, cl. ii. div. A. filza iii, fo. 169: 'una caccia in tavola dell'istessa lunghezza, alta un palmo, di mano antichissima et eccellente'). The panel is well preserved; the high lights apparent in reproduction in the foliage on the right-hand side are due to old flaking. The use of foreground trees to divide the picture surface into mathematically equal parts connects the design with that of the San Martino 'Nativity'.

THE FOUNDERS OF FLORENTINE ART
Louvre, Paris, No. 1272.
PLATES 107–12
Panel: 42×210 cm.
Collection Louis Philippe; Stevens (sale 1847).

Vasari, in the first edition of the *Vite* (i, 1550, pp. 290–1) attributes the painting, which was at that time in the house of the architect Giuliano da Sangallo, to Masaccio: 'Et che e mostro col giudizio suo quasi che per vn testamento in cinque teste fatte da lui, a chi per lo augumento fatto nelle arti, si avesse ad avere il grado di quelle: Lasciandocene in una tauola di sua mano, oggi in casa Giuliano da San Gallo in Fiorenza, i ritratti quasi uiuissimi, che sono questi: GIOTTO per il principio della pittura: DONATO per la scultura: FILIPPO Brunellesco per la archittura: & PAVLO VCCELLO, per gli animali, & per la Prospettiua. Et tra questi, ANTONIO Manetti, per eccellentissimo Matematico de' tempi suoi.' In the second and subsequent editions (ed. Milanesi, 1906, ii, pp. 213–14) Vasari describes the panel in the life of Uccello in the following terms: 'Amo Paulo, sebbene era persona stratta le virtu degli artefici suoi; e perche ne rimanesse ai posteri memoria, ritrasse di sua mano, in una tavola lunga, cinque uomini segnalati, e la teneva in casa per memoria loro: l'uno era Giotto pittore, per il lume e principio dell'arte: Filippo di ser Brunelleschi il secondo, per l'architettura: Donatello per la scultura: e se stesso per la prospettiva ed animali: e per la matematica Giovanni Manetti suo amico, con quale conferiva assai e ragionava delle cose di Euclide.' The panel appears to have enjoyed some celebrity in the sixteenth century, when the head of Donatello was adapted in a panel now in the Museo Civico at Padua (No. 422. Panel: 21·1×15·7 cm. Moschetti, 'Un ritratto ignorato di Donatello', in *Bollettino del Museo Civico di Padova*, xi, 1908, pp. 174–7), that of Giotto in a panel formerly in the Pozzi collection, London, and those of Giotto, Donatello and Brunelleschi in a version on canvas in the Fitzwilliam Museum, Cambridge (22·6×64·2 cm.), ascribed by Richter (*The Mond Collection*, ii, 1910, p. 477) to Francesco Salviati; in this the heads are combined with portraits of Raphael and Michelangelo.

The inscriptions beneath the portraits date from the (?) sixteenth century, and there is thus no certainty as to the persons represented. If Vasari's first description is correct, the panel represents not, as Boeck and other writers have suggested, the discoverers of perspective, but the founders of Florentine art, and shows, from left to right, the painter Giotto, Uccello, the sculptor Donatello and on the extreme right the architect Brunelleschi. Whether the second head from the right purports to represent Brunelleschi's biographer Antonio di Tuccio Manetti (b. 1423), as assumed by Milanesi (in Vasari, *Vite*, ii, p. 216n.) or Antonio di Ciaccheri detto Manetti (b. 1405), as supposed by Boeck (*Paolo Uccello*, 1939, p. 130), is contingent on the date at which the painting is presumed to have been made. An intarsia worker, Antonio Manetti, is listed among the masters of perspective in the *Memorie*

Catalogue

storiche di Benedetto Dei (Bibl. Riccardiana, No. 1853, printed by Semper, *Donatello*, in *Quellenschriften für Kunstgeschichte*, ix, 1875, p. 263). Boeck ('Uccello Studien', in *Zeitschrift für Kunstgeschichte*, ii, 1933, pp. 145–7) suggests that the heads represent, from left to right, Uccello, Brunelleschi, Donatello, Manetti, and Giotto; Lanyi ('The Louvre Portrait of five Florentines', in *The Burlington Magazine*, lxxxiv–v, 1944, pp. 94–5) identifies the heads, from left to right, as Masaccio, Uccello (or an anonymous figure), Donatello, Manetti and Brunelleschi. In the absence of established portraits of these artists (other than the death-mask of Brunelleschi discussed by Poggi, 'La "maschera" di Filippi Brunelleschi nel Museo dell'Opera del Duomo', in *Rivista d'Arte*, xii, 1930, pp. 533–40, and the putative self-portrait of Masaccio in the 'St. Peter enthroned', illustrated in reverse by Lanyi, op. cit., Pl. iii), no reasonable degree of certainty as to the identity of the five sitters can be attained. The arguments against the view that the figure on the left, which wears the dress of the 1420s and has some of the character of a self-portrait, represents Giotto, are insuperable. Analogies for the panel are to be found in a triple portrait of the Gaddi family in the Uffizi, in which one of the three heads is copied from a fresco by Agnolo Gaddi, and in a quadruple portrait at Munich (Gronau, 'Eine deutsche Kopie nach Domenico Ghirlandaio im Münchner National Museum', in *Münchner Jahrbuch für Bildende Kunst*, i, 1906, pp. 109–12), derived from four heads in the foreground of Domenico Ghirlandaio's 'Sacrifice of Zacharias' in Sta Maria Novella; and there are strong reasons for supposing that the heads in the present panel are assembled from one or more prototypes. This case is argued by Richter (loc. cit.), who supposed that this panel and the version in the Fitzwilliam Museum had a common prototype in portraits of distinguished artists decorating the 'rooms in which members of the Guild of Painters met'; and by Schmarsow ('Zur Masolino-Masaccio Forschung', in *Zeitschrift für Bildende Kunst*, lxiv, 1930–1, p. 3) and Lanyi (loc. cit.), who suggest that the heads derive from Masaccio's lost fresco of the 'Sagra del Carmine'. In this fresco Masaccio is stated by Vasari (ed. cit., ii, p. 295) to have represented Brunelleschi, Donatello, Masolino, and a number of other portraits, some of which were repeated 'di mano del medesimo in casa di Simon Corsi'. Lanyi rests his case on the facts (i) that the figures depicted in the Louvre panel are of different sizes, (ii) that two of the artists whose names appear on the Louvre panel, are known to have been depicted in the 'Sagra del Carmine', and (iii) that the heads in the Louvre panel are lit, as they would have been lit in the fresco, from the right, and not from the left. If, however, the heads derived from the 'Sagra del Carmine', which was known to Vasari in the original, it is inexplicable that he should not have recognized their source. While the connexion with the 'Sagra del Carmine' is hypothetical, the conclusion can hardly be avoided that the heads derive from one or more frescoed prototypes.

Solutions of the problem of the authorship of the Louvre panel fall into three categories. The first supposes that the panel is by, or associable with, Masaccio; the second that it is by, or associable with, Uccello; the third that it was painted in the sixteenth century. In favour of the first view are Beenken ('Zum Werke des Masaccio, I', in *Zeitschrift für Bildende Kunst*, lxiii, 1929, pp. 112–19), who believes the panel to be an autograph work by Masaccio of 1426–8, and Lanyi (loc. cit.), who regards it as an anonymous quattrocento derivative from Masaccio's fresco. Longhi (*Piero della Francesca*, 1947, p. 157) now concurs in this view. In favour of the second view are Berenson (*Italian Pictures of the Renaissance: Florentine School*, 1963, p. 209, and earlier editions), Boeck (op cit., pp. 111–12), who had earlier postulated a collaboration between Masaccio and Uccello ('Die "Erfinder" der Perspektive', in *Repertorium für Kunstwissenschaft*, lii, 1931, pp. 143–7), Horne ('The Battle-piece by Uccello in the National Gallery', in *The Monthly Review*, 1901, October, p. 114), Lipman ('The Florentine Profile Portrait in the Quattrocento', in *The Art Bulletin*, xviii, 1936, p. 101), who lists the painting as 'Shop of Paolo Uccello', Van Marle (*The Development of the Italian Schools of Painting*, x, 1928, p. 298), Pudelko ('Florentiner Porträts der Frührenaissance', in *Pantheon*, xv, 1935, p. 98), Salmi (*Paolo Uccello, Andrea del Castagno, Domenico Veneziano*, 1938, pp. 147–8), Sindona (*Paolo Uccello*, 1957, pp. 37, 55) and Carli (*Tutta la pittura di Paolo Uccello*, 1959, pp. 29–30, 60–1). Shell ('The Early Style of Fra Filippo Lippi and the Prato Master', in *The Art Bulletin*, xliii, 1961, p. 205 and n.) mistakenly ascribes the panel to the same hand as the 'Trivulzio Madonna' in Milan (Museo del Castello Sforzesco) and postulates a somewhat earlier dating than other students. Schubring (*Cassoni*, 1923, p. 105), believes the panel to have been repainted in the sixteenth century by Bugiardini. In favour of the third view are Crowe and Cavalcaselle (op. and ed. cit., iv, p. 119), who appear to have considered the picture 'an old copy of the time of Pontormo', and Benkard (*Das Selbstbildnis*, 1927, pp. 47–9). There is a high degree of probability that we have here to do with a work produced in the fifteenth century modified by later repainting. In view of the factor of condition, and of the possibility that two or more heads are copied from Masaccio, the matter of attribution is more than usually difficult, but the fact remains that the panel is more closely associable with Uccello than with any other artist. A point of reference for the head inscribed as Uccello's is, as Boeck (op. cit., p. 33) points out, to be found in the frescoes round the clock in the Duomo, while those of the figure known as Giotto, the Manetti, and the much damaged Brunelleschi find general parallels in 'Noah's Sacrifice' and 'The Drunkenness of Noah' in the Chiostro Verde. On the other hand, the style of the representations is not closely related to that of Uccello's only authenticated portrait, the head of Niccolò da Tolentino in the National Gallery 'Rout of San Romano'. Boeck ('Die "Erfinder" der Perspektive' in *Repertorium für Kunstwissenschaft*, lii, 1931, pp. 143–7) proposes datings about 1425, and later (*Paolo*

Uccello, 1939, pp. 34–5) a dating about 1436–43. Other critics, among them Schubring (op. cit., p. 242), Pudelko (op. cit., p. 98), Salmi (loc. cit.), Berenson (op. cit., p. 500) and Lipman (op. cit., p. 101), are in agreement that the painting, if by Uccello, is a late work, certainly executed after 1450 and possibly after 1460. No valid solution of the problems to which it gives rise can be advanced in the present state of the painting. Plates 109 and 111 show the panel before, and Plates 107, 108, 110 and 112 after, restoration.

OTHER WORKS ASCRIBED TO UCCELLO

I. MOSAICS

THE BIRTH OF THE VIRGIN, THE PRESENTATION OF THE VIRGIN IN THE TEMPLE, and THE VISITATION
Cappella Mascoli, San Marco, Venice.

Figs. XVII, XVIII.

The presence of Uccello in Venice is attested by a passage in a tax return of 1427 (Florence, Archivio di Stato, Archivio delle Decime, Quartiere di San Giovanni Gonfalone Drago, 1427, vol. 55, fol. 707 r. and v., printed by Boeck, *Paolo Uccello*, 1939, p. 96): 'Andossi con Dio più di II anni fa ed e a Vinegia'. If, as this passage states, Uccello left Florence for Venice in 1425, his arrival may have been connected with the decision of the Venetian Senate on 11 March 1424 to seek a master mosaicist to undertake or superintend work in San Marco (Saccardo, *Les mosaïques de Saint Marc*, 1897, p. 33). Muraro ('L'esperienza veneziana di Paolo Uccello', in *Atti del XVIII congresso internazionale di storia dell'arte*, Venice, 1956, pp. 197–200) suggests that the demand for Uccello's services resulted from the need to repair damage caused in the fire of 1419. We know that Uccello was employed as a master mosaicist at San Marco, since on 23 March 1432 the Operaii of the Duomo in Florence instructed the Florentine orator at Venice to ascertain 'de quodam Paolo Doni de Florentia, magistro musayci, qui Venetiis laboravit in facie s. Marci a parte exteriore unam figuram s. Petri in quodam angulo faciei s. Petri suttus orilgium de anno domini 1425, tempore cujus erant operarii dominus Leonardus Mozanighi et dominus Marinus, utrum bene laboravit prefatam et cuius est in civitate Venetiarum extimationis et pretii et an de vitreis potest haberi et reperiri et cuius pretii sunt, de quibus omnibus placeat eorum officium reddere advisatum' (Florence, Archivio dell'Opera del Duomo, Deliberazioni, 1425–36, f. 156 v., printed by Poggi, *Il Duomo di Firenze*, 1909, No. 773). The figure of St. Peter executed by Uccello in 1425 has disappeared (see below), but a plausible attempt is made by Muraro (loc. cit.) to establish his authorship of a number of geometrical roundels on the roof and pavement of the

XVII. GIAMBONO: THE BIRTH OF THE VIRGIN AND THE PRESENTATION OF THE VIRGIN IN THE TEMPLE. *San Marco, Venice*

XVIII. GIAMBONO: THE VISITATION. *San Marco, Venice*

church, as well as of a head of a warrior removed from a mosaic of the Magi in the Baptistry, adjacent to the Zen Chapel, which is now in the Museo di San Marco. Recurrent efforts to link Uccello's name with the decoration of the Mascoli Chapel, the most important of the mosaics put up in the interior of the basilica in these years, have been inconclusive. The matter is analysed by Muraro ('The Statutes of the Venetian Arti and the Mosaics of the Mascoli Chapel', in *The Art Bulletin*, xliii, 1961, pp. 263–74) in the light of Venetian guild practices. The altar of the Mascoli chapel was dedicated in 1430. Uccello's intervention in the mosaics was first postulated by Longhi ('Lettere pittoriche', in *Vita Artistica*, i, 1926, pp. 129–30), in connexion with the upper part of the architectural setting of 'The Visitation'. Pudelko ('The Early Works of Paolo Uccello', in *The Art Bulletin*, xvi, 1934, pp. 253–4) subsequently advanced the view that Uccello was responsible for the initial cartoons of 'The Birth of the Virgin' and 'The Presentation of the Virgin in the Temple', and that these were modified by Giambono, who signed the mosaic. This thesis has since been accepted by Longhi ('Fatti di Masolino e di Masaccio', in *Critica d'Arte*, xxv–vi, 1940, p. 179), who, however, limits Uccello's responsibility to the architecture of the 'Presentation' and regards the figures as the work of Giambono. Pudelko's attribution presents many difficulties, and while the architecture of the 'Visitation' is, as Longhi claims, superficially Tuscan in character, there is nothing to connect it firmly with Uccello. Moreover, it is questionable whether any of the mosaics in the chapel were designed before 1432. Giambono's authorship of the three mosaics is accepted by Hartt ('The earliest Works of Andrea del Castagno, II', in *The Art Bulletin*, xli, 1959, p. 231). Work on the mosaics is known to have been in progress in 1444 (Thode, in *Festschrift für Otto Benndorf*, 1898, p. 315), and a dating about 1440 is consistent with what we know of Giambono's style. Salmi (*Paolo Uccello, Andrea del Castagno, Domenico Veneziano*, 1938, pp. 144–5) ascribes the architecture of 'The Visitation' to Jacopo Bellini. A summary reproduction of Uccello's lost mosaic of St. Peter is identified by Salmi ('Riflessioni su Paolo Uccello', in *Commentari*, i, 1950, pp. 22–3) in Gentile Bellini's 'Procession of the Reliquary of the Cross'. This convincing identification is accepted by Sindona (*Paolo Uccello*, 1957, pp. 24–5), who also recognizes Uccello's presence in mosaics of San Bernardino and St. Paul, two heads of Warriors, and three rose-pattern designs. Hartt ('The earliest Works of Andrea del Castagno, I', in *Art Bulletin*, xli, 1959, p. 167) comments that 'Uccello left far more extensive examples of his style and his ideas among the mosaics of St. Mark's than merely the lost St. Peter'. The San Bernardino and St. Paul are signed by a Maestro Antonio, and are not closely related to the St. Peter.

II. PAINTINGS

SERAPH
Sta Trinita, Florence.

Three scenes from the life of St. Francis painted by Uccello in Sta Trinita are described by Vasari (*Vite*, ed. Milanesi, ii, 1906, p. 206): 'e in Santa Trinita, sopra alla porta sinistra dentro alla chiesa, in fresco, storie di San Francesco: cioè il ricevere delle stimate, il riparare alla chiesa reggendola con le spalle, e lo abboccarsi con San Domenico'. These frescoes, the attribution of which to Uccello goes back to Manetti and Albertini, are also mentioned by Baldinucci (*Notizie de' Professori del Disegno*, ii, 1768, p. 132) as being 'sopra la porta di mezzo'. Pudelko ('Studien über Domenico Veneziano', in *Mitteilungen des Kunsthistorischen Instituts in Florenz*, iv, 1934, p. 157n.) identifies a much damaged Seraph on the entrance wall of the church as a fragment of Uccello's lost 'Stigmatization of St. Francis'. The interest of this fragment in its present state is archaeological.

ADAM AND EVE EXPELLED FROM PARADISE and THE LABOURS OF ADAM AND EVE: THE SACRIFICES OF CAIN AND ABEL and THE MURDER OF ABEL.

THE BLIND LAMECH KILLING HIS GREAT-GRANDFATHER and THE BUILDING OF THE ARK: THE ANIMALS ENTERING THE ARK
Sta Maria Novella (Chiostro Verde), Florence.

Figs. XIX, XX.

The frescoes fill the two bays of the east wall of the Chiostro Verde adjacent to that on which Uccello's early frescoes are set. 'The Expulsion from Paradise' (but not the remaining frescoes) is ascribed to Uccello by the *Libro di Antonio Billi* and the Anonimo Magliabechiano (see note to Plates 1–2 above), followed by Crowe and Cavalcaselle (*A History of Painting in Italy*, iv, 1911, p. 112), who also differentiate between the frescoes in the second and those in the third bay. Van Marle (*The Development of the Italian Schools of Painting*, x, 1928, p. 230) gives both bays to the School of Uccello. The four frescoes, all of which are by one and the same hand, have a generic relationship to the earlier frescoes of Uccello, but are of lower quality and contain elements which are not directly Uccellesque. Lanyi ('Quercia-Studien', in *Jahrbuch für Kunstwissenschaft*, 1930, pp. 54–5) is perhaps justified in

XIX. DELLO DELLI (?): ADAM AND EVE EXPELLED FROM PARADISE and THE LABOURS OF ADAM AND EVE. *Chiostro Verde, Santa Maria Novella, Florence*

XX. DELLO DELLI (?): THE BLIND LAMECH KILLING HIS GREAT-GRANDFATHER and THE BUILDING OF THE ARK. *Chiostro Verde, Santa Maria Novella, Florence*

XXI. THE PRATO MASTER: THE BIRTH OF THE VIRGIN. *Duomo, Prato*

XXII. THE PRATO MASTER: THE PRESENTATION OF THE VIRGIN IN THE TEMPLE. *Duomo, Prato*

XXIII. THE PRATO MASTER: THE DISPUTE OF SAINT STEPHEN. *Duomo, Prato*

tracing the influence of Quercia's San Petronio reliefs on the 'Expulsion'. The style of the frescoes is analysed by Salmi ('Aggiunte al trecento e quattrocento fiorentino', in *Rivista d'Arte*, xvi, 1934, pp. 168–86) and Pudelko ('The Minor Masters of the Chiostro Verde', in *The Art Bulletin*, xvii, 1935, pp. 71–6). By the latter the frescoes are ascribed to Dello Delli and dated 1446–8. Salmi (*Paolo Uccello, Andrea del Castagno, Domenico Veneziano*, 1938, pp. 146–7) correctly points out that this late dating is untenable. It is likely that the frescoes were executed not long after Uccello's scenes in the first bay, and if by Dello Delli they must date before the artist left for Spain in 1433.

SCENES FROM THE LIVES OF THE VIRGIN AND ST. STEPHEN
Duomo, Prato.
Figs. XXI, XXII, XXIII.

The fresco cycle in the Cappella dell'Assunta to the right of the Cappella Maggiore in the Cathedral at Prato consists (i) of representations of Faith, Hope, Charity, and Fortitude, on the roof of the chapel, (ii) of a number of single figures of saints on the arch of the entrance to the chapel, (iii) of three frescoes on the

right wall of the chapel showing (from top to bottom) the 'Birth of the Virgin', the 'Presentation of the Virgin in the Temple', and the 'Marriage of the Virgin', and (iv) of three frescoes on the left wall of the chapel showing (from top to bottom) the 'Dispute of St. Stephen', the 'Stoning of St. Stephen', and the 'Finding of the Body of St. Stephen'. The frescoes are by two separate hands, the first responsible for (i), (ii), the top fresco on the left and the two upper frescoes on the right wall, and the second for the two lower frescoes on the left and for the bottom fresco on the right wall. The second of these artists has been convincingly identified with Andrea di Giusto, whose death in 1450 provides a *terminus ante quem* for the completion of the lower frescoes. According to normal practice, the execution of the frescoes on the upper part of the two walls would have preceded those below. A *terminus post quem* for the upper frescoes is provided by Uccello's clock-face in the Duomo at Florence (1443), which appears to have influenced the types in the 'Dispute of St. Stephen' and the 'Presentation of the Virgin in the Temple'. Pudelko ('Der Meister der Anbetung in Karlsruhe', in *Das siebente Jahrzehnt: Festschrift zum 70. Geburtstag von Adolf Goldschmidt*, 1935, p. 125n.) notes the presence of figures painted by Andrea di

Other Works Ascribed to Uccello

Giusto in the background of 'The Presentation in the Temple'. The history of the chapel, which was at one time wrongly known as the Cappella Bocchineri but appears to have been founded in 1418 by the wife of Giovanni di Francesco di Ruffolo, affords no indication of the date of the frescoes (Salmi, 'Paolo Uccello, Domenico Veneziano, Piero della Francesca e gli affreschi del Duomo di Prato', in *Bollettino d'Arte*, xxviii, 1934–5, pp. 1–16). But the fact that reflections of the style of the lower scenes appear in the work of the Sienese painter Pietro di Giovanni d'Ambrogio suggest that they may have been completed before the death of this artist in 1448. Baldanzi (*La Cattedrale di Prato*, 1846, p. 47n.) publishes a protest addressed by the Canons of the Cathedral to the Proposto (1447) at the removal of the stained glass in the Chapel two years earlier. It is accepted by Marchini (*Il Duomo di Prato*, 1957, pp. 77–85) that this may have been done to provide light for the painting of the frescoes. Ragghianti ('Intorno a Filippo Lippi', in *Critica d'Arte*, iii, 1938, pp. xxiv–v) appears to favour a dating prior to 1445, and is followed in this by Sindona (*Paolo Uccello*, 1957, p. 34, ca. 1442–4), Carli (*Tutta la pittura di Paolo Uccello*, 1959, pp. 22 f., soon after 1436), and Berti ('Una nuova Madonna e degli appunti su un grande maestro', in *Pantheon*, xix 1961, p. 302, between 1436 and 1443). The upper frescoes have been attributed (i) to Domenico Veneziano (Schmarsow, 'Domenico Veneziano', in *L'Arte*, xv, 1912, pp. 81 ff.), (ii) to Uccello (Longhi, 'Fatti di Masolino e di Masaccio', in *La Critica d'Arte*, xxv–vi, 1940, p. 179), and (iii) to an unidentified Uccellesque painter alternatively identified with Giovanni di Francesco (Longhi, 'Ricerche su Giovanni di Francesco', in *Pinacoteca*, i, 1928, pp. 40–4. Berenson, *Italian Pictures of the Renaissance*, Florentine School, 1963, p. 58), the Master of the Karlsruhe 'Adoration' (Pudelko, loc. cit.) and the Master of the Quarata Predella (Salmi, loc. cit.). The attribution to Domenico Veneziano does not warrant serious discussion, though Pudelko (op. cit., p. 126) suggests that the 'Birth of the Virgin', at Prato derives from the lost fresco of the same scene painted by Domenico Veneziano in S. Egidio in Florence in 1439–45, and Sindona (op. cit., p. 33) suggests that Domenico Veneziano visited Prato to work on the frescoes. An attribution to Uccello is maintained by Berti (op. cit., p. 300) and Carli (loc. cit.), and is contested by Marchini (op. cit., p. 82) and Shell ('The Early Style of Fra Filippo Lippi and the Prato Master', in *The Art Bulletin*, xliii, 1961, p. 206). Marchini distinguishes between the author of the frescoes and the painter of the Dublin Madonna (see below), while Shell accepts this grouping. Before the removal of the frescoes from the wall of the chapel, the rudimentary treatment of space throughout the scenes seemed to militate against a direct attribution to Uccello, and to be inconsistent with the complex perspective scheme of the clock-face of 1443. The form and handling of the *sinopia* revealed beneath the 'Birth of the Virgin' (*Mostra di affreschi staccati*, Fortezza di Belvedere, Florence, 1966) is wholly incompatible with

those of the *sinopie* beneath Uccello's frescoes. The quality of the upper scenes, though much superior to that of the lower frescoes, is appreciably below the level of Uccello's authenticated work. On the other hand the Uccellesque character of the style, as defined initially by Longhi, is undeniable, and it is clear that we have here to do with an animated, mannered and deeply individual painter trained in Uccello's studio prior to 1443. It is possible that the paintings associable with the Karlsruhe 'Adoration' (q.v.) represent a different phase of the same artist; there is, however, no clear evidence of this.

An unconvincing attempt is made by Shell (loc. cit.) to ascribe to the same hand the fresco of 'The Confirmation of the Carmelite Rule' (formerly in the cloister of the Carmine), the 'Trivulzio Madonna' (Museo del Castello Sforzesco, Milan) and a 'Madonna and Saints' at Empoli. The latter is certainly and the two former paintings are probably by Fra Filippo Lippi.

BEATO JACOPONE DA TODI
Sala del Capitolo, Duomo, Prato.

Fresco transferred to canvas: 180 × 60 cm.

The fresco was discovered behind a later altar in the Chapel of the Assumption in 1871, and was removed from the wall and transferred to the Sala Capitolare at this time (for this see Marchini, *Il Duomo di Prato*, 1957, pp. 77–85). It is by the same artist as the 'Scenes from the Life of the Virgin' in the same chapel (see above). It was exhibited, under an ascription to Uccello, at the *Mostra di quattro maestri del primo rinascimento* (Palazzo Strozzi, Florence, 1954, No. 22), and its attributional vicissitudes follow those of the main frescoes. It is ascribed by Kaftal (*The Iconography of the Saints in Tuscan Painting*, 1952, p. 504) to an anonymous Uccellesque master.

VIRGIN AND CHILD
National Gallery of Ireland, Dublin, No. 603.
Fig. XXIV.

Panel: 57 × 33 cm.

Extensive retouching in the right half of the Virgin's face and on the right cheek of the Child. The Virgin's robe is dark blue and the niche light grey, with a pinkish-red cornice behind the Virgin's head.

Bardini sale, London, 5 June 1899, No. 357, as Lorentino d'Andrea; Butler; Langton Douglas. A Florentine origin for the painting is postulated by Fry ('The Umbrian Exhibition at the Burlington Fine Arts Club', in *The Burlington Magazine*, xvi, 1909–10, p. 274), who ascribes it to a follower of Domenico Veneziano. The attribution to Uccello is due to Pudelko ('An unknown Holy Virgin Panel by Paolo Uccello', in *Art in America*, xxiv, 1936, pp. 127–34). Pudelko bases the ascription on the geometrical forms used throughout the panel and on resemblances between the form of the pointed ears of the Child and those of the head of Micheletto Attendoli da Cotignola in the Louvre 'Rout of San Romano'. The appearance of a supposed copy of the

XXIV. THE PRATO MASTER: MADONNA AND CHILD.
National Gallery of Ireland, Dublin

type of the Virgin in the Uccellesque frescoes at Prato
implies for Pudelko a dating before 1445. A tentative
attribution to Uccello is also proposed by Salmi (*Paolo
Uccello, Andrea del Castagno, Domenico Veneziano*,
1938, pp. 145–6). The panel was shown, under an
attribution to Uccello, at the *Mostra di quattro maestri del
primo rinascimento* (Palazzo Strozzi, Florence, 1954, No.
15) and at the Centenary Exhibition of the National
Gallery of Ireland (1964, No. 4). It is accepted as an
autograph work of Uccello by Sindona (*Paolo Uccello*,
1957, pp. 34, 59, dated ca. 1445), Carli (*Tutta la pittura
di Paolo Uccello*, 1959, pp. 22, 27–8, 58, as shortly before
1450) and Berti ('Una nuova Madonna e degli appunti su
un grande maestro', in *Pantheon*, xix, 1961, p. 303, with
a dating ca. 1436–43). The panel is omitted from the
Uccello catalogue of Boeck. The style context of the
Dublin 'Madonna' is that of the Prato frescoes, and in
view of resemblances, e.g. between the head of the
Child and the head of a youthful female figure with
loose hair in the decorative framing, there can be no
doubt that it was executed by the Prato Master rather
than by Uccello. This case is accepted by Shell ('The
early Style of Fra Filippo Lippi and the Prato Master',
in *The Art Bulletin*, xliii, 1961, p. 208) and rejected by
Marchini (*Il Duomo di Prato*, 1957, p. 82). The panel
appears to date from after 1440.

XXV. THE PRATO MASTER: A FEMALE SAINT WITH
TWO CHILDREN. *Contini-Bonacossi collection, Florence*

A FEMALE SAINT WITH TWO CHILDREN
Contini-Bonacossi collection, Florence.
Fig. XXV.

Panel: 79 × 35 cm.

Fragment from the right side of an altar-piece. The
robe of the principal figure is black, and the architecture behind her pink.
Published by Longhi ('Ricerche su Giovanni di
Francesco', in *Pinacoteca*, i, 1928–9, p. 44) as Giovanni

Other Works Ascribed to Uccello

di Francesco. Longhi identifies the Saint as St. Scholastica, and points to analogies with the Prato frescoes and, in the case of the two child portraits, with the kneeling Saints in the 'Adoration' at Karlsruhe. Salmi (*Paolo Uccello, Andrea del Castagno, Domenico Veneziano*, 1938, p. 24) and Pudelko ('An unknown Holy Virgin Panel by Paolo Uccello', in *Art in America*, xxiv, 1936, pp. 128, 133) as Uccello, the former with a dating about 1440, the latter somewhat later. According to Salmi and Pudelko, this ascription has been endorsed verbally by Longhi. Uccello's authorship of the panel is endorsed by Sindona (*Paolo Uccello*, 1957, p. 34, ca. 1445), Carli (*Tutta la pittura di Paolo Uccello*, 1959, pp. 21-2, 57, ca. 1440), and Berti ('Una nuova Madonna e

degli appunti su un grande maestro', in *Pantheon*, xix, 1961, pp. 300, 303). It is listed by Berenson (*Italian Pictures of the Renaissance: Florentine School*, 1963, p. 88) as a work of Giovanni di Francesco. Boeck (*Paolo Uccello*, 1939, p. 120) supports an ascription of Oertel to the Master of the 'Scenes from the Life of St. Benedict' in the Chiostro degli Aranci of the Badia. The attribution of the panel is inseparable from that of the Dublin 'Madonna' (as noted by Pudelko) and of the Prato frescoes (as noted by Longhi), and both the principal figure and the rather tentative handling of the architecture behind find parallels in the 'Presentation of the Virgin' at Prato. The panel appears to date from about 1445-55.

XXVI–XXVIII. THE PRATO MASTER: SAINT JOHN ON PATMOS; THE ADORATION OF THE MAGI; TWO KNEELING SAINTS; *Museo Diocesano di Castello, Florence*

SAINT JOHN ON PATMOS, THE
ADORATION OF THE MAGI, and TWO
KNEELING SAINTS

*Museo Diocesano di Castello, Florence (from San
Bartolommeo a Quarata, Bagno a Ripoli).*

Figs. XXVI, XXVII, XXVIII.

Panel: 20·5 × 178 cm.

The three panels, which form the predella of a lost
altar-piece, were published after cleaning by Marangoni
('Una predella di Paolo Uccello', in *Dedalo*, xii, 1931–2,
pp. 329–46) as early works of Uccello, datable between
1426 and 1432. An early dating ca. 1425 is accepted by
Sindona (*Paolo Uccello*, 1957, pp. 22 f., 57). The ascription to Uccello is sustained by Serra (in *Bollettino
d'Arte*, xxvii, 1933–4, p. 45), Ragghianti ('Intorno a
Filippo Lippi', in *Critica d'Arte*, iii, 1938, p. xxiv),
and Boeck (*Paolo Uccello*, 1939, pp. 74–5), who claims
that analogies for the style of the panels are to be found
in late works by Uccello, the Ashmolean 'Hunt' and
the Urbino predella. Longhi ('Fatti di Masolino e di
Masaccio', in *La Critica d'Arte*, xxv–vi, 1940, p. 179)
also accepts Marangoni's ascription to Uccello, but
proposes a somewhat later dating (1445–50), and is
followed in this by Carli (*Tutta la pittura di Paolo
Uccello*, 1959, pp. 22, 58) and Berti (*Paolo Uccello*, in
I Maestri del Colore). The panels are given by Berenson
(*Italian Pictures of the Renaissance*, 1932, p. 342 and
later editions) to the Master of the Carrand Triptych
(Giovanni di Francesco). Though Gamba ('La Mostra
del Tesoro di Firenze Sacra', in *Bollettino d'Arte*, xxvii
1933–4, p. 155) correctly observes that certain elements
in the predella (notably its colour) derive from other
sources than Uccello, its style is generically Uccellesque,
and it is accepted as the work of an anonymous
Uccellesque Master by Lauts (*Katalog Alter Meister*,
Karlsruhe, 1966, p. 187) and Kaftal (*The Iconography
of the Saints in Tuscan Painting*, 1952, p. 59). Kaftal
identifies the Saint on the extreme right as Ansanus.
The attempt of Pudelko ('Der Meister der Anbetung
in Karlsruhe', in *Das siebente Jahrzehnt: Festschrift
zum 70. Geburtstag von Adolf Goldschmidt*, 1935, pp.
126–7) to ascribe the panels to the Master of the
Karlsruhe 'Adoration' is rejected by Giovanozzi ('Note
su Giovanni di Francesco', in *Rivista d'Arte*, xvi, pp.
360–1n.). Salmi ('Paolo Uccello, Domenico Veneziano,
Piero della Francesca e gli affreschi del Duomo di
Prato', in *Bollettino d'Arte*, 1934–5, pp. 1–16), associates them with the Prato frescoes, and proposes a
dating shortly before 1445. This grouping is very
plausible, and is supported by clear analogies between
figures in the 'Adoration of the Magi' and in the Prato
'Dispute of St. Stephen'. The influence of Fra Angelico
which is evident in the central scene of the predella, is,
however, absent from the Prato frescoes. A direct
ascription to Uccello is untenable, as is the assumption
that the predella presupposes knowledge of Uccello's
late work. The panels appear to have been produced
about 1440–50.

XXIX. THE KARLSRUHE MASTER: THE ADORATION
OF THE CHILD. *Staatliche Kunsthalle, Karlsruhe*

THE ADORATION OF THE CHILD,
WITH SAINTS JEROME, MARY
MAGDALEN AND EUSTACE

Staatliche Kunsthalle, Karlsruhe, No. 404.
Fig. XXIX.

Panel: 110 × 47 cm.

Associated with the studio of Uccello by Loeser ('Paolo
Uccello', in *Repertorium für Kunstwissenschaft*, xxi,

Other Works Ascribed to Uccello

1898, pp. 89–90) and Gamba ('Di alcuni quadri di Paolo Uccello o della sua scuola', in *Rivista d'Arte*, vi, 1909, pp. 19–30). Subsequent opinion in respect of the panel is divided between those who follow Schmarsow (*Kunsthistorische Gesellschaft für Photographische Publikationen*, vi, 1900, p. 5, Pls. xxv–xxvi), Longhi ('Ricerche su Giovanni di Francesco', in *Pinacoteca*, i, 1928, pp. 42–3), Berenson (*Italian Pictures of the Renaissance*, 1932, p. 342, and later editions), and Offner ('The Mostra del Tesoro di Firenze Sacra', in *Burlington Magazine*, lxiii, 1933, p. 177n.) in ascribing it to a hypothetical early phase of the Master of the Carrand Triptych (Giovanni di Francesco), and those who, with Pudelko ('Der Meister der Anbetung in Karlsruhe', in *Das siebente Jahrzehnt: Festschrift zum 70. Geburtstag von Adolf Goldschmidt*, 1935, pp. 123–30), regard it as the nucleus of an independent personality, influenced by Uccello and perhaps trained in Uccello's studio. The arguments against Giovanni di Francesco's authorship of the panel are concisely stated by Giovannozzi ('Note su Giovanni di Francesco', in *Rivista d'Arte*, xvi, 1934, p. 356). The following paintings are ascribed to the Master of the Karlsruhe 'Adoration' by Pudelko:

> Bagno a Ripoli, S. Bartolommeo a Quarata: Predella
> Boston, Gardner Museum: 'Portrait of a Lady'
> Florence, Accademia: 'Scenes from Monastic Legends'
> Lugano, Thyssen collection: 'Christ on the Cross with four Saints'
> Paris, Musée Jacquemart-André: 'St. George and the Dragon'
> Prato, Duomo: Frescoes in Cappella dell'Assunta
> Prato, Palazzo Communale: 'Cardinal Niccolò da Prato'
> New York, Bache Collection: 'Portrait of a Lady'
> Art market (1928): Wing of Triptych
> Art market: 'Virgin and Child with Angels' (repr. Van Marle, 'Eine Madonna von Paolo Uccello', in *Pantheon*, ix, 1932, pp. 375 ff.)

This list contains (i) two works by the same hand as the Karlsruhe 'Adoration', the Thyssen 'Christ on the Cross' and the Accademia 'Scenes from Monastic Legends'; (ii) two works by an independent Uccellesque painter, the Prato frescoes and the Bagno a Ripoli predella; (iii) a panel from the workshop of Uccello, the Jacquemart-André 'St. George'; and (iv) two works by an unidentified artist, the Bache and Gardner portraits. The panel in the Palazzo Communale at Prato is not immediately Uccellesque. Also by the Master of the Karlsruhe 'Adoration' are a 'Madonna' in the National Gallery of Art at Washington, a 'Madonna' in Berlin, and a 'Christ carrying the Cross' in the Congregazione di Carità at Parma (q.v.): Lauts (*Meisterwerke der Staatlichen Kunsthalle Karlsruhe*, 1957, p. 44, No. 38, and *Katalog Alte Meister*, Karlsruhe, 1966, pp. 187–8, No. 404) accepts the integrity of a group comprising the Karlsruhe 'Adoration', the Accademia 'Scenes from Monastic Legends', the Thyssen 'Crucifixion', and the Parma 'Christ carrying the Cross'. Pudelko endeavours to trace the

hand of the Karlsruhe Master in the frescoes in the cloister of San Miniato, and it is not impossible that this artist was responsible for the frescoes on the south wall of the cloister; these frescoes are now too severely damaged for satisfactory analysis. The surviving works of the master seem to date between about 1440 (Karlsruhe 'Adoration') and about 1460 (Accademia 'Thebaid'). The picture was shown in 1954 under an attribution to Uccello at the *Mostra di quattro maestri del primo rinascimento* (Palazzo Strozzi, Florence, No. 19), and un untenable ascription to Uccello is retained by Sindona (*Paolo Uccello*, 1957, p. 22, dated before 1425) and Parronchi ('Due note para-uccellesche', in *Arte antica e moderna*, No. 30, 1965, p. 178).

VIRGIN AND CHILD
North Carolina Museum of Art, Raleigh, N.C.
(*Kress collection. K 518*).
Fig. xxx.

Panel: 58 × 41 cm.

Coll.: Chiesa, Milan; Contini-Bonacossi, Florence.

The catalogue of the National Gallery of Art (*Preliminary Catalogue of Paintings and Sculpture*, 1941, p. 201) states that the panel is associated by A. Venturi, Suida and Perkins with the Prato frescoes, and is given by Berenson to a Paduan follower of Uccello. The

XXX. THE KARLSRUHE MASTER: MADONNA AND CHILD. *North Carolina Museum of Art, Raleigh, N.C.* (*Kress collection*)

168

XXXI. THE KARLSRUHE MASTER: MADONNA AND CHILD WITH ST. FRANCIS AND TWO ANGELS. *Allentown Art Museum, Allentown, Pa. (Kress collection)*

painting, which is much abraded, is by the same hand as, and is closely related to, a damaged 'Virgin and Child' in Berlin (see below). The picture is catalogued by Shapley and Suida (*The Samuel H. Kress Collection: North Carolina Museum of Art*, Raleigh, 1960, p. 58) as 'Circle of Paolo Uccello', and by Shapley (*Italian Paintings from the Samuel H. Kress Collection, Italian Schools XIII–XV century*, 1966, pp. 101–2) as 'Attributed to Paolo Uccello', and was shown at the *Mostra di quattro maestri del primo rinascimento* (Palazzo Strozzi, Florence, 1954, No. 24) under an attribution to Uccello. It is accepted as a work of Uccello by Berti ('Una nuova Madonna e degli appunti su un grande artista', in *Pantheon*, xix, 1961, pp. 300, 303), who dates it at the time of the fresco of 'The Drunkenness of Noah'. The possibility of Uccello's authorship of this and of the Berlin painting can be ruled out. In both the type of the Child, with its elongated body, is related to that in the Karlsruhe 'Adoration'.

VIRGIN AND CHILD
Private collection, Florence.
Panel.
The panel is published by Berti ('Una nuova Madonna e degli appunti su un grande maestro', in *Pantheon*, xix, 1961, pp. 298–308) as Uccello. A radiograph

reproduced in this article shows that its surface is considerably damaged and has been extensively restored. The painting is inseparable in style from the Berlin and Raleigh 'Madonnas', and like them is by the Karlsruhe Master.

VIRGIN AND CHILD WITH ST. FRANCIS AND TWO ANGELS
Allentown Art Museum, Allentown (Pa.) (Kress collection. K 320).
Fig. XXXI.

Panel: 60·3 × 45·8 cm.

Coll.: Contini-Bonacossi, Florence.

Published by Ragghianti ('Argomenti lippeschi e uccelleschi', in *Miscellanea minore di critica d'arte*, 1946, p. 75, fig. 6) as Uccello, and ascribed by Salmi ('Riflessioni su Paolo Uccello', in *Commentari*, i, 1950, p. 26) to the Master of the Quarata Predella, the picture was catalogued in 1951 by Suida (*Paintings and Sculpture from the Kress Collection*, National Gallery of Art, Washington, 1951, No. 10, p. 44) as 'Florentine School, ca. 1440, possibly Uccello'. Shapley (*Paintings and Sculpture from the Kress Collection*, Allentown Art Museum, 1960, p. 48) lists written opinions from

XXXII. THE KARLSRUHE MASTER (?): MADONNA AND CHILD WITH TWO ANGELS

Other Works Ascribed to Uccello

Longhi (as Uccello), Suida (as close to or by Uccello), Fiocco and Van Marle (as close to Uccello), Perkins and A. Venturi (as an unidentified master) and Berenson (as possibly Romagnole). The panel is accepted as a work of Uccello by Berti ('Una nuova Madonna e degli appunti su un grande maestro', in *Pantheon*, xix, 1961, p. 303), who dates it about 1450 and compares the angels to those in Sassetta's 'Mystic Marriage of St. Francis' at Chantilly. The painting, which was cleaned in 1960, is by the Karlsruhe Master.

VIRGIN AND CHILD
T. S. Hyland collection, Greenwich (Connecticut).

Panel: 47 × 34 cm.

Coll.: Rev. J. Shine, Dublin; Sestieri, Rome.

This panel, in which the Virgin and Child are shown against a landscape, was unrecorded before its appearance at the *Mostra di quattro maestri del primo rinascimento* (Palazzo Strozzi, No. 24bis), when it was stated by Micheletti (p. 61) to have been accepted as a work of Uccello by Longhi, Toesca and Salmi. The attribution to Uccello is endorsed by Berti ('Una nuova Madonna e degli appunti su un grande maestro', in *Pantheon*, xix, 1961, p. 304), who regards it as a late work. This ascription cannot be maintained. Parronchi ('Due note para-uccellesche', in *Arte antica e moderna*, No. 30, 1965, p. 178) gives the work to Uccello's daughter,

'Soror Antonia'. The type of the Child suggests that we have here to do with a late work by the Karlsruhe Master. The painting is, however, inferior in quality to the Madonnas by this hand at Raleigh and in Berlin. It is ascribed by Berenson (*Italian Pictures of the Renaissance: Florentine School*, 1963, p. 87) to Giovanni di Francesco.

VIRGIN AND CHILD WITH TWO ANGELS
Private collection.
Fig. XXXII.
Panel.

Coll.: Carl Hamilton, New York (1938).

This panel, in which the Child stands on a parapet and the figures are set against a landscape, was first published as a work of Uccello by Van Marle ('Eine Madonna von Paolo Uccello,' in *Pantheon*, ix, 1932, pp. 76-80). The attribution was contested in the first edition of this book (p. 162), where doubt was wrongly cast on the authenticity of the panel, and is rejected by Carli (*Tutta la pittura di Paolo Uccello*, 1959, p. 70). Uccello's authorship of the panel has since been re-affirmed by Berti ('Una nuova Madonna e degli appunti su un grande maestro,' in *Pantheon*, xix, 1961, pp. 304–7). The painting is inseparable from the Hyland Madonna, and is a damaged work of the same date by the same hand.

XXXIII. THE KARLSRUHE MASTER: CHRIST ON THE CROSS WITH THE VIRGIN, SAINT FRANCIS AND THE TWO SAINTS JOHN. *Thyssen collection, Lugano*

XXXIV. THE KARLSRUHE MASTER: MADONNA AND CHILD. *Bode Museum, East Berlin.*

VIRGIN AND CHILD

Bode Museum, East Berlin (Inv. No. 1470).
Fig. XXXIV.

Panel: 60 × 42 cm.

Officially designated as Paduan School, the painting was ascribed to Uccello by Ragghianti ('Intorno a Filippo Lippi', in *Critica d'Arte*, iii, 1938, p. xxiv). The attribution to Uccello appears to have been supported verbally by Valentiner (for this see Shapley, *The Samuel H. Kress Collection: North Carolina Museum of Art*, Raleigh, 1960, p. 58) and is maintained by Berti ('Una nuova Madonna e degli appunti su un grande maestro', in *Pantheon*, xix, 1961, p. 303) with a dating ca. 1443. As noted in the first edition of this book, the panel is by the same hand as a 'Virgin and Child' formerly in the National Gallery of Art, Washington (Kress collection), now in the North Carolina Museum of Art, Raleigh N.C. (q.v.), and both paintings are by the Karlsruhe Master. The gold ground has been renewed.

CHRIST ON THE CROSS WITH THE VIRGIN AND SAINTS JOHN BAPTIST, JOHN EVANGELIST AND FRANCIS

Thyssen collection, Lugano.
Fig. XXXIII.

Panel: 46 × 67·5 cm.

Attributed to Uccello by Van Marle ('Eine Kreuzigung von Paolo Uccello', in *Pantheon*, i, 1928, p. 242; and

The Development of the Italian Schools of Painting, x, 1928, pp. 210–14), and accepted as a work of Uccello by Boeck (*Paolo Uccello*, 1939, pp. 14–16, 110), Marangoni ('Una predella di Paolo Uccello', in *Dedalo*, xii, 1931–2, p. 334), Salmi (*Paolo Uccello, Andrea del Castagno, Domenico Veneziano*, 1938, p. 41) L. Venturi ('Paolo Uccello', in *L'Arte*, xxxiii, 1930, p. 63). Sindona (*Paolo Uccello*, 1957, p. 23), Carli (*Tutta la pittura di Paolo Uccello*, 1959, pp. 48, 64) and Berti ('Una nuova Madonna e degli appunti su un grande maestro', in *Pantheon*, xix, 1961, pp. 300, 304). The panel, evidently the centre-piece of a predella, is regarded by Boeck, Marangoni and Sindona as an early and by Salmi, Carli and Berti as a late work. As with the 'Scenes from Monastic Legends' in the Accademia the dating in the 1420s proposed by Boeck is inadmissible irrespective of the authorship of the panel. Along with the Accademia painting, the panel is referred by Berenson (*Italian Pictures of the Renaisance*, 1932, p. 342) to the Master of the Carrand Triptych (Giovanni di Francesco) and by Pudelko ('Der Meister der Anbetung in Karlsruhe', in *Das siebente Jahrzehnt: Festschrift zum 70. Geburtstag von Adolf Goldschmidt*,

XXXV. THE KARLSRUHE MASTER: CHRIST CARRYING THE CROSS. *Congregazione di Carità S. Filippo Neri, Parma*

XXXVI. THE KARLSRUHE MASTER: SCENES FROM MONASTIC LEGENDS. *Accademia, Florence*

1935, p. 127) to the Master of the Karlsruhe 'Adoration'. The many dissentient views on the authorship of the panel are ignored by Heinemann (*Sammlung Schloss Rohoncz*, 1958, p. 110, No. 431). The present panel, the 'Adoration' and the painting in the Accademia are closely inter-related in style, and it is illogical to attempt, with Salmi, to introduce one of the three paintings in isolation into Uccello's œuvre. In the case of the 'Crucifixion' the relatively low quality of drawing and execution affords a decisive argument against an ascription to Uccello. The panel seems to date from the sixth decade of the century.

CHRIST CARRYING THE CROSS
Congregazione di Carità S. Filippo Neri, Parma, No. 10.
Fig. XXXV.

Panel: 53 × 34 cm.

According to Micheletti (*Mostra di quattro maestri del primo rinascimento*, 1954, p. 58), the picture was acquired in Florence in 1786 by Marchese Tacoli-Canacci under an attribution to Castagno.
The ascription of Berenson (*Italian Pictures of the Renaissance*, 1932, p. 342) to the Master of the Carrand Triptych (Giovanni di Francesco) is rejected by Giovannozzi ('Note su Giovanni di Francesco', in *Rivista d'Arte*, xvi, 1934, p. 360) in favour of an

attribution to the Prato Master, in which Salmi ('Riflessioni su Paolo Uccello', in *Commentari*, i, 1950, p. 26) concurs. The treatment of the figure and robe is, however, more closely related to that of the St. Jerome in the lower part of the Karlsruhe 'Adoration' and to the Accademia 'Thebaid', and the panel, which was cleaned in 1947, was certainly executed by the Karlsruhe Master. On the cartellino are the words: . . . SEMETIP-SUM ET TOLLAT CRUCEM SVAM ET SEQV . . . ME.

SCENES FROM MONASTIC LEGENDS
Accademia, Florence, No. 5381.
Fig. XXXVI.
Linen or canvas: 81 × 110 cm.

From Santo Spirito alla Costa San Giorgio.
Transferred to the Accademia in 1808.

The painting, which is sometimes incorrectly described as a 'Thebaid', shows in the foreground on the left the Virgin appearing to St. Bernard, in the centre two unidentified scenes, and on the right St. Romuald (?) teaching; in the background on the left is an unidentified scene showing a number of flagellants kneeling before the crucified Christ and a layman exhorted by a friar or monk, and in the centre are the stigmatization of St. Francis and St. Jerome before a crucifix.
The painting was first associated with the studio of

Uccello by Gamba ('Di alcuni quadri di Paolo Uccello o della sua scuola', in *Rivista d'Arte*, vi, 1909, p. 19), and its connexion with Uccello has since been unanimously recognized. A direct ascription to the artist is proposed by Boeck ('Ein Frühwerk von Paolo Uccello', in *Pantheon*, viii, 1931, p. 276, and *Paolo Uccello*, 1939, pp. 10–14, 110), and has since been accepted by Marangoni ('Una predella di Paolo Uccello', in *Dedalo*, xii, 1931–2, pp. 335, 337), Longhi, Sindona (*Paolo Uccello*, 1957, pp. 20, 57, as Uccello's earliest work) and Berti ('Una nuova Madonna e degli appunti su un grande maestro', in *Pantheon*, xix, 1961, p. 304, as contemporary with the predella at Urbino). Whatever the authorship of the painting, Boeck's very early dating (prior to 1420) is unacceptable, and the panel, despite its superficially archaic scheme, can hardly have been produced before the middle of the century. Paatz (*Die Kirchen von Florenz*, ii, 1941, p. 167) dates it ca. 1445. Salmi (*Paolo Uccello, Andrea del Castagno, Domenico Veneziano*, 1938, pp. 154–6) notes that the rainbow in the centre background and the figure of St. Romuald derive from the later frescoes in the Chiostro Verde, and that the painting must therefore post-date these works. The use of canvas is in itself an argument in favour of a relatively late dating. Gamba (loc. cit.) correctly identifies the artist with the Master of the Karlsruhe 'Adoration', a view subsequently endorsed by Pudelko ('Der Meister der Anbetung in Karlsruhe', in *Das siebente Jahrzehnt: Festschrift zum 70. Geburtstag von Adolf Goldschmidt*, 1935, pp. 124–5) and Giovannozzi ('Note su Giovanni di Francesco', in *Rivista d'Arte*, xvi, 1934, p. 356). Parronchi ('Le Fonti di Paolo Uccello', in *Studi su la dolce prospettiva*, 1964, pp. 523–4, 526) explains the painting as 'una riassuntiva illustrazione' of the *De Oculo Morali* of Pierre Lacepierre de Limoges, and advances 'una sentimental ipotesi', that the painting was executed by Uccello's daughter Antonia (1456–91), a Carmelite nun who was also a 'pittoressa'. Pudelko (loc. cit.) suggests that the scenes may derive from the lost frescoes stated by the Anonimo Magliabechiano (*Il Codice Magliabechiano*, herausgegeben von Carl Frey, 1892, p. 100: 'et anchora nel munisterio de fratj dellj Agnolj nel chiostretto dall'orto dipinse di uerde terra molte fiure, con grande artifitio et tenute dallj intendentj assaj rare') to have been executed by Uccello in the Monastero degli Angeli. These frescoes are, however, said by Vasari (see below) to have represented scenes from the life of St. Benedict.

XXXVII. VENETIAN SCHOOL: A FEMALE SAINT. *San Gottardo, Asolo*

THE DEAD CHRIST BETWEEN THE VIRGIN AND ST. JOHN EVANGELIST
Soprintendenza alle Gallerie, Florence (formerly Oratorio dell'Annunziata, Avane).

Fig. XXXVIII.

Panel: 22 × 177 cm.

The predella of a lost altar-piece, the panel, which has suffered serious paint losses, is ascribed by Longhi ('Fatti di Masolino e di Masaccio', in *La Critica d'Arte*, v, 1940, p. 179) to Uccello. This attribution is sustained by Micheletti (*Mostra di quattro maestri del primo rinascimento*, 1954, No. 21), Sindona (*Paolo Uccello*, 1957, pp. 37, 60), Carli (*Tutta la pittura di Paolo Uccello*, 1959, p. 60) and Berti ('Una nuova Madonna e degli appunti su un grande maestro', in *Pantheon*, xix, 1961, pp. 300, 303). The affinities of the panel are with the work of the Prato Master. The date 1452 inscribed on this predella is the single firm indication of the chronology of this artist's works.

XXXVIII. THE PRATO MASTER: THE DEAD CHRIST BETWEEN THE VIRGIN AND SAINT JOHN EVANGELIST. *Soprintendenza alle Gallerie, Florence*

Other Works Ascribed to Uccello

THE CRUCIFIXION
Pinacoteca, Ravenna, No. 191.

Panel: 37 × 27 cm.

Published by Schmarsow (*Kunsthistorische Gesellschaft für Photographische Publikationen*, vi, 1900, p. 5, Pl. xvii) as a putative early work by Uccello. The panel (for which see Martini, *La Galleria dell' Accademia di Ravenna*, 1959, pp. 111–12) is in the style of Lorenzo Monaco, to whom it is ascribed by Berenson (*Italian Pictures of the Renaissance: Florentine School*, 1963, p. 121) and other students.

A FEMALE SAINT
San Gottardo, Asolo.

Fig. XXXVII.

The ascription of this fresco fragment to Uccello is due to Fiocco ('Un affresco di Paolo Uccello nel Veneto', in *Bollettino d'Arte*, iii, 1923–4, p. 193, as Uccello; *Mantegna*, 1937, p. 196, as style of Uccello). The fragment is connected by Longhi ('Lettere pittoriche' in *Vita Artistica*, i, 1926, p. 132) with Antonio Vivarini, and is regarded by Salmi (*Paolo Uccello, Andrea del Castagno, Domenico Veneziano*, 1938, p. 144) and Procacci ('Gherardo Starnina', in *Rivista d'Arte*, xvii, 1935, p. 381) as Venetian. There is no reason to associate this figure with Uccello.

MALE FIGURE
Palazzo Ducale, Venice (Sala del Piovego).

This fragmentary fresco is doubtfully identified as a work of Uccello of the late fourteen-twenties by Muraro ('L'esperienza veneziana di Paolo Uccello', in *Atti del XVIII congresso internazionale di storia dell'arte*, Venice, 1956, pp. 197–200).

CAESAR'S VICTORY OVER THE GAULS
Graf Lanckoronski, Vienna (formerly).

Panel: 42 × 151 cm.

Regarded by Schubring (*Cassoni*, 1915, pp. 241–2, No. 100) as the single battle-scene on a cassone panel for which an attribution to Uccello is admissible. The style of the panel derives from Pesellino, and is not immediately Uccellesque.

EPISODES FROM THE MYTH OF THESEUS
Seattle Art Museum, Seattle, Washington (Kress collection. K 480).

Panel: 41 × 156·2 cm.

Coll.: Mameli, Rome; Contini-Bonacossi, Florence.

The panel is given by Shapley (*Paintings from the Samuel H. Kress Collection: Italian Schools, XIII–XV Century*, 1966, pp. 102–3) to a follower of Paolo Uccello, and seems to originate in the same studio as the panel noted above.

III. DRAWINGS

The following drawings, over and above those discussed in the body of this book, have been ascribed to Uccello:

Bergamo, Accademia Carrara. 'Two Heads of Horses' (Fig. 6). The attribution to Uccello is due to Frizzoni (*Collezione di Quaranta Disegni scelti della raccolta del senatore Giovanni Morelli*, 1886). The drawing is North Italian.

Berlin, Kupferstichkabinett, No. 5047. 'Kneeling Shepherd and two seated Women'. Boeck ('Drawings by Paolo Uccello', in *Old Master Drawings*, viii, 1933–4, Pl. 1; *Paolo Uccello*, p. 126) as Uccello. Berenson (*The Drawings of the Florentine Painters*, 1938, No. 2772) links this drawing with six sheets by the same hand in the Uffizi, Florence, as works of the school of Paolo Uccello, with the tentative suggestion that they should be looked upon as 'copies made by a pupil after early sketches by Uccello'. The style of the drawings is no more than generically Uccellesque, and a direct ascription to Uccello either for these sheets or for their presumed originals cannot be maintained.

Florence, Uffizi (Gabinetto dei Disegni, No. 1107E). 'A seated and a standing male Nude'. Boeck (op. cit., Pl. 2; *Uccello*, p. 126) and Sindona (*Paolo Uccello*, 1957, p. 36) as Uccello. Berenson (op. cit., No. 2776) as by the same hand as the preceding drawing.

Florence, Uffizi (Gabinetto dei Disegni, No. 14508F). 'Male Nude with arms raised.' The sheet is listed by Berenson (op. cit., No. 2779C) as School of Paolo Uccello, and is given by Sindona (*Paolo Uccello*, 1957, p. 36) to Uccello.

Florence, Uffizi (Gabinetto dei Disegni, No. 1302F). 'Angel' (probably for an 'Expulsion from Paradise'), Fig. XXXIX. Boeck (op. cit., Pl. 3; *Uccello*, p. 128), Salmi (*Paolo Uccello, Andrea del Castagno, Domenico Veneziano*, 1938, p. 152) and Berti (*Paolo Uccello*, 1964, fig. 2, in *I Maestri del Colore*). Sindona (*Paolo Uccello*, 1957, pp. 43, 61) 'conferma la attribuzione con riserva' as Uccello. Berenson (op. cit., No. 2778C) as perhaps by the Carrand Master. Salmi correctly refers the style of the drawing to that of the Urbino predella. Perhaps, as suggested by Pudelko ('Der Meister der Anbetung in Karlsruhe', in *Das siebente Jahrzehnt: Festschrift zum 70. Geburtstag von Adolf Goldschmidt*, 1935, p. 128), by the Master of the Karlsruhe 'Adoration'.

Two drawings of male heads in profile in the Albertina

XXXIX. STYLE OF UCCELLO: AN ANGEL. *Uffizi, Florence*

XL. AFTER UCCELLO (?): HEAD OF A MAN
Albertina, Vienna, S.R. 52

XLI. AFTER UCCELLO (?): HEAD OF A MAN
Albertina, Vienna, S.R. 53

XLII. STUDIES FROM THE 'LIBRO DE' DISEGNI' OF VASARI
ASCRIBED TO UCCELLO. *National Museum, Stockholm*

at Vienna (S.R. 52, 53) (Figs. XL, XLI) are regarded by Berenson (op. cit., Nos. 2780, 2780A) as copies after lost drawings by Uccello.

For the student of Uccello some importance attaches to a group of drawings at Stockholm (Fig. XLII) and Vienna, originating from the *Libro de' Disegni* of Vasari, where they were ascribed to the artist. These sheets are listed by Kurz ('Giorgio Vasari's *Libro de' Disegni*', in *Old Master Drawings*, xii, 1937–8, pp. 9–10). The individual sheets are discussed by Sirén (*Italienska Handteckningar*, 1917, pp. 5–9). None of them can any longer be regarded as a candidate for inclusion among Uccello's works, but the drawings of animals, which predominate, may well have coloured certain pages of Vasari's narrative. A number of the animal drawings are referred by Kurz tentatively to the School of Pisanello. It cannot, however, be assumed that all drawings representing animals are necessarily North Italian; and comparison of the sheets with the fantastic animals in the first of the Chiostro Verde frescoes suggests that they may represent a lost class of drawing by Uccello.

LOST WORKS BY UCCELLO

FLORENCE
Convent of Annalena.
'Two Figures.'

Two unidentified figures (for which see Paatz, *Die Kirchen von Florenz*, v, 1953, pp. 411, 414) painted in fresco on an external wall of the cloister of the convent of Annalena are ascribed to Uccello in the *Codice Magliabechiano* (*Il Codice Magliabechiano*, ed. Frey, 1892, pp. 99–100: 'Nella faccia del munistero delle suore di Baldaccio ovvero Annalena fece due fiure') and in the *Libro di Antonio Billi* (*Il Libro di Antonio Billi*, ed. Frey, 1892, p. 25: 'Fece due fiure nella faccia del munistero di Annalena'). The cloister was built in 1455, and the frescoes must date from after this time.

FLORENCE
Chiostro degli Angeli.
'Scenes from the Life of St. Benedict.'

Frescoes by Uccello in the cloister of the Convento degli Angeli are mentioned by the *Codice Magliabechiano* (ed. cit., pp. 99–100: 'Et anchora nel munistero de fratj dellj Agnolj nel chiostretto dall'orto dipinse di uerde terra molte fiure, con grande artifitio et tenute dallj intendentj assaj rare') and the *Libro di Antonio Billi* (ed. cit., p. 25: 'Dipinse negli Angioli nel chiostro dellato [dell'orto] grande di uerde terra di molto fiure, assai lodato'). These references are amplified by Vasari (*Vite*, ed. Milanesi, ii, 1906, p. 213): 'Lavoro anco di colore di verde terra la loggia che e volta a ponente sopra l'orto del monastero degli Angeli; cioe sotto ciascun arco una storia de' fatti di San Benedetto abbate, e delle più notabili cose della sua vita insino alla morte; dove, fra molti tratti che vi sono bellissimi, ve n'ha uno, dove un monastero per opera del demonio rovina; e sotto i sassi e legni rimane un frate morto. Ne e manco notabile la paura di un altro monaco, che fuggendo ha i panni che, girandi intorno all'ignudo, svolazzano con bellissima grazia: nel che desto in modo l'animo agli artefici, che eglino hanno poi seguitato sempre questa maniera. E bellissima ancora la figura di San Benedetto, dove egli con gravita e devozione, nel cospetto de' suoi monaci risuscita il frate morto. Finalmente, in tutte quelle storie sono tratti da essere considerati; e massimamente in certi luoghi, dove sono tirati in prospettiva infine agli embrici e tegoli del tetto. E nella morte di San Benedetto, mentre i suoi monaci gli fanno l'esequie e lo piangono, sono alcuni infermi e decrepiti a vederlo, molto belli. E da considerare ancora che, fra molti amorevoli e divoti di quel Santo, vi e un monaco vecchio con due gruccie sotto le braccia, nel quale si vede un affetto mirabile, e forse speranza di riaver la sanita. In questa opera non sono paesi di colori, ne molti casamenti o prospettivo difficili; ma si bene gran disegno, e del buono assai.' It is probable that in this last sentence Vasari wished to contrast the uniform tonality of the frescoes and their relatively simple visual schemes with those of the frescoes at San Miniato. The suggestion of Salmi ('Riflessioni su Paolo Uccello', in *Commentari*, i, 1950, p. 28) that a sheet in the Uffizi (No. 97E), showing four seated monks, ascribed by Berenson (*The Drawings of the Florentine Painters*, ii, 1938, No. 168) to the School of Fra Angelico, reproduces a detail from the frescoes in the Chiostro degli Angeli, is unconvincing.

FLORENCE
Carmine.
'SS. Cosmas and Damian.'

A dossal or antependium painted by Uccello is recorded by Vasari in the Carmine (*Vite*, ed. Milanesi, ii, p. 208: 'Dopo dipinse nel Carmine, nella cappella di San Girolamo dei Pugliesi, il dossale di San Cosimo e Damiano'). The painting (for which see Paatz, *Die Kirchen von Florenz*, iii, 1952, p. 232) is likely to have been destroyed in the fire of 1771. Since the Pugliesi chapel was frescoed by Starnina, it is argued by Salmi

Lost Works

(*Paolo Uccello, Andrea del Castagno, Domenico Veneziano*, 1938, pp. 9, 101, 133) that Uccello's painting must have been an early work. An attempt to identify two panels of SS. Cosmas and Damian in Berlin (Nos. 1141C, 1141D) as parts of Uccello's lost dossal is rejected by Pudelko (in Thieme *Künsterlexikon*, xxxiii, 1939, p. 526). According to Parronchi ('Due note parauccellesche', in *Arte antica e moderna*, No. 30, 1965, p. 179n.), the dossal from the Pugliesi chapel is to be identified with a celebrated painting of the 'Thebaid' in the Uffizi (No. 447), which would therefore be a work of Uccello of about 1431. There is no substance in this attribution.

FLORENCE
Sta Maria Maggiore.
'The Annunciation.'

Albertini (*Memoriale di molte statue e pitture della citta di Firenze fatto da Francesco Albertini*, 1863, p. 12) describes in the church of Santa Maria Maggiore 'una tavola di Masaccio: la predella e lo archo di sopra e di Paolo Uccello'. The altar-piece in question is a disassembled altar-piece by Masolino. A detailed description of the work above it is given in the second edition of Vasari's *Lives* (*Vite*, ed. and vol. cit., pp. 206–7): 'Lavoro ancora in Santa Maria Maggiore in una cappella, allato alla porta del fianco che va a San Giovanni, dove e la tavola e predella di Masaccio, una Nunziata in fresco: nella qual fece un casamento degno di considerazione, e cosa nuova e difficile in quei tempi, per essere stata la prima che si mostrasse con bella maniera agli artefici, e con grazia e proporzione, mostrando il modo di fare sfuggire le linee, e fare che in un piano lo spazio che e poco e piccolo, acquisti tanto che paia assai lontano e largo; e coloro che con giudizio sanno a questo con grazia aggiugner l'ombre a' suoi luoghi ed i lumi con colori, fanno senza dubbio che l'occhio s'inganna, che pare che la pittura sia viva e di rilievo. E non gli bastando questo, volle anco mostrare maggiore difficulta in alcune colonne che scortano per via di prospettiva, le quali ripiegandosi rompono il canto vivo della volta, dove sono i quattro Evangelisti; la qual cosa fu tenuta bella e difficile.' Paatz (*Die Kirchen von Florenz*, Frankfurt-am-Main, 1952, iii, pp. 630, 653–4) concludes that Uccello's 'Annunciation' was painted in fresco on the wall above the altar-piece by Masolino. The fresco is last mentioned by Baldinucci, and is assumed to have been destroyed after 1650 when authority was granted to the Carmelite friars to demolish the Carnesecchi altar of which it formed part. An 'Annunciation' ascribed to Uccello is, however, mentioned by Richa (*Notizie storiche delle chiese fiorentine*, iii, 1755, p. 281: 'ne si dee tralasciare di dire per compimento di quel poco, che abbiamo osservato, come di queste, ne restano a potersi vedere alquante, cioe una Nunziatina di Paolo Uccello al primo pilastro nell'entrare a mano manco'). From this it is inferred by Parronchi ('Una Nunziatina di Paolo Uccello: Ricostruzione della Cappella Carnesecchi', in *Studi su la dolce prospettiva*, Milan, 1964, pp. 182–225) that

Uccello's 'Annunciation' was painted on panel, and is identical with the so-called 'Goldman Annunciation' by Masolino in the National Gallery of Art in Washington. It may be noted in this connection (i) that Vasari's testimony is too explicit to admit of any theory other than that Uccello's 'Annunciation' was a fresco, (ii) that the 'Goldman Annunciation' is an indubitable work by Masolino, (iii) that it is too large to be described as 'una Nunziatina', and (iv) the passage in Richa proves only that in the eighteenth century a small panel of the Annunciation ascribed to Uccello existed in the church. In view of its connection with the Masolino altar-piece Uccello's fresco of 'The Annunciation' can only be regarded as a very early work. It is suggested by Pudelko ('The early Works of Paolo Uccello', in *The Art Bulletin*, xvi, 1934, pp. 243–4) that the composition is reproduced in an 'Annunciation' by Paolo Schiavo in the Collegiata at Castiglione d'Olona, and by Spencer ('Spatial Imagery of the Annunciation in fifteenth-century Florence, in *The Art Bulletin*, xxxvii, 1955, p. 275) that it represented a traditional 'Annunciation' iconography akin to that of Fra Angelico and Lorenzo Monaco, and not the advanced iconography of Masaccio's lost 'Annunciation' in S. Niccolò.

FLORENCE
S. Miniato al Monte.
'Christ on the Cross.'

Saalman ('Paolo Uccello at San Miniato', in *The Burlington Magazine*, cvi, 1964, pp. 559–60 and 563. Doc. VII) publishes a document of 12 February 1455 (1454st, fior.), in which Uccello, working with an assistant, Antonio di Papi, is credited with twenty-one florins 'per dipintura duna facciata in refettorio nuovo conuno crocifisso et conuno fregio intorno et uno fregio dapie adetta facciata con cierte figure'. There is no trace of paintings in either the former refectory or the former chapter hall.

FLORENCE
S. Pier Coelorum.
'St. Andrea Corsini.'

A payment made to Uccello on 30 June 1453, refers to the painting of a figure of the Blessed Andrea Corsini in the Library of the Cathedral. The relevant document (for which see Boeck, *Paolo Uccello*, 1939, p. 103) reads: 'pro parte sui magisterii unius figure beati Andree picte in Libreria'. This work (for which see Paatz, *Die Kirchen von Florenz*, iv, 1952, pp. 619, 620) is noted by Milanesi (Vasari, *Vite*, ed. Milanesi, 1906, ii, p. 211n.). Andrea Corsini was beatified in 1439.

FLORENCE
S. Tommaso.
'Christ and St. Thomas.'

A fresco of 'Christ and St. Thomas' above the entrance to the church of San Tommaso is mentioned in the

Codice Magliabechiano (ed. cit., pp. 99–100: 'Et sopra la porta della chiesa di Santo Tomaso in merchato vecchio dipinse Cristo e San Tomaso') and the *Libro di Antonio Billi* (ed. cit., p. 25: 'et sopra la porta di Santo Tommaso di Firenze Cristo et Santo Tommaso'). The story which Vasari (ed. and vol. cit., pp. 216–17) embroiders round this, Uccello's 'ultima fatica', reads: 'Dicesi che, essendogli dato a fare sopra la porta di San Tommaso in Mercato Vecchio lo stesso Santo che a Cristo cerca la piaga, che egli mise en quell' opera tutto lo studio che seppe, dicendo che voleva mostrar in quella quanto valeva e sapeva: cosi fece fare una serrata di tavole, accio nessuno potesse vedere l'opera sua se non quando fusse finita. Perche, scontrandolo un giorno Donato tutto solo, gli disse: E che opera fia questa tua, che cosi serrata la tiene? Al quale respondendo Paulo disse: Tu vedrai, e basta. Non lo volle astringer Donato a dir piu oltre, pensando, come era solito, vedere quando fusse tempo, qualche miracolo. Trovandosi poi una mattina Donato per comperare frutte in Mercato Vecchio, vide Paulo che scopriva l'opera sua; perche salutandolo cortesemente, fu dimandato da esso Paulo, che curiosamente desiderava udirne il giudizio suo, quello che gli apresse di quella pittura. Donato, guardato che ebbe ben bene, disse: Eh, Paolo; ora che sarebbe tempo di coprire, e tu scopri! Allora, constristandosi Paolo grandemente, si senti avere di quella sua ultima fatica molto piu basimo, chenon aspettava di averne lode.'

FLORENCE
Sta Trinità.
'Scenes from the Life of St. Francis.'

See under 'Other Works ascribed to Uccello'.

FLORENCE
Spedale di Lemmo.
'St. Anthony the Abbot between SS. Cosmas and Damian.'

The attribution of this lost fresco to Uccello goes back to Vasari (ed. and vol. cit., p. 206): 'Le pitture prime di Paulo furono in fresco, in una nicchia bislunga tirata in prospettiva nello spedale di Lemmo; cioè un Sant' Antonio Abate, e San Cosimo e Damiano che lo mettono in mezzo'. This passage is repeated by Baldinucci (ed. and vol. cit., p. 132), who appears not to have known the fresco. Vasari's reference to the presence of a perspective niche suggests that the fresco may have belonged to the same early phase of Uccello's development as the 'Hawkwood'.

FLORENCE
Casa Bartolini.
'Four Battle-pieces.'

See note on 'The Rout of San Romano' above.

FLORENCE
Palazzo Medici.
'Battle of Dragons and Lions: Scene from the Legend of Paris.'

See note on 'The Rout of San Romano' above.

There is a conflict of evidence between the account of these paintings given in the Medici inventory of 1492 (see p. 150), where they are described as representing one 'battaglie & draghj et lionj' and the other 'della storia diparis' (presumably the Judgement of Paris), and the account given by Vasari (ed. and vol. cit., p. 208): 'E in detta casa, fra l'altre storie d'animali, fece alcuni leoni che combattevano fra loro, con movenze e fierezze tanto terribili, che parevano vivi. Ma cosa rara era, fra l'altre, una storia, dove un serpente combattendo con un leone mostrava con movimento gagliardo la sua fierezza ed il veleno che gli schizzava per bocca e per gli occhi; mentre una contadinella, ch'e presente, guarda un bue fatto in iscorto bellissimo, del quale n'e il disegno proprio di mano di Paulo nel nostro Libro de' disegni: e similmente della villanella, tutta piena di paura e in atto di correre, fuggendo dinanzi a quegli animali. Sonovi similmente certi pastori molto naturali, ed un paese che fu tenuto cosa molto bella nel suo tempo.' The second of the paintings described by Vasari can hardly be identical with the scene from the legend of Paris (unless some scene other than the Judgement was represented), and it must therefore be the 'battle of dragons and lions' mentioned in the inventory. The first of the paintings described by Vasari is perhaps that by Pesellino.

An attempt is made by Salmi ('Riflessioni su Paolo Uccello', in *Commentari*, i, 1950, pp. 29–33) to isolate in a number of engravings datable between about 1460 and 1490 motifs presumed to have derived from the lost paintings by Uccello and Pesellino in the Palazzo Medici. The engravings in question are those listed by Hind (*Early Italian Engraving*, i, 1938) as:

A.II.2	Florentine about 1460.	*Beasts and Birds hunting and fighting*
A.II.3	Florentine about 1460.	*Wild Animals attacking Horses and Oxen*
A.II.17	Florentine about 1470.	*A Bear Hunt*
A.IV.24	Florentine about 1465–80.	*A Bear Hunt*
D.III.4	Lucantonio degli Uberti.	*Lion, Lioness and Dragon fighting*
E.III.12	Venetian (?) about 1470–90.	*Lion, Dragon and Fox quarrelling*

These engravings are of interest as indicating the class of composition to which the lost paintings belonged, rather than as evidence of the schemes employed.

FLORENCE
Casa Peruzzi.
Painted Ceiling.

Vasari (ed. and vol. cit., p. 215): 'Lavoro Paulo, in fresco, la volta de' Peruzzi a triangoli in prospettiva; ed in su i cantoni dipinse, nelle quadrature, i quattro elementi, ed a ciascuno fece un animale a proposito: alla terra una talpa, all'acqua un pesce, al fuoco la salamandra, ed all'aria il camaleonte che ne vive e piglia ogni colore. E perche non ne aveva mai veduti, fece un cammello che apre la bocca ed inghiottisce aria, empiendosene il ventre.'

Lost Works

PADUA
Casa Vitaliani.
'Giants.'

The earliest account of these frescoes occurs in the Anonimo Morelliano (ed. Frimmel, in *Quellenschriften für Kunstgeschichte*, n.f. 1, pp. 28–9): 'Alli Heremitani in casa delli Vitelliani. Li Giganti di chiaro et scuro furono de mano de Paulo Uccello Fiorentino, che li fece un al giorno per precio de ducato 'no 'luno.' The frescoes are also mentioned by Vasari (ed. and vol. cit. p. 214): 'Fu condotto Paulo da Donato a Padova, quando vi lavoro; e vi dipinse nell'entrata della casa de' Vitali, di verde terra, alcuni giganti, che (secondo ho

XLIV. NICCOLÒ PIZZOLO: GIGANTIC HEAD.
Eremitani, Padua

XLIII. LEONARDO DA BESOZZO: PAGE FROM AN ILLUMINATED CHRONICLE. *Crespi-Morbio collection, Milan*

trovato in una lettera latina che scrive Girolamo Campagnola a M. Leonico Tomeo filosofo) sono tanto belli, che Andrea Mantegna ne faceva grandissimo conto.' A number of drawings of Old Testament and other figures in the *Chronicle* of Leonardo da Besozzo (Crespi-Morbio collection, Milan) (Fig. XLIII), in which Toesca (*La pittura e la miniatura nella Lombardia*, 1912, p. 486) first noted the influence of Uccello, are regarded by Fiocco ('I Giganti di Paolo Uccello' in *Rivista d'Arte*, xvii, 1935, p. 385) as adaptations of Uccello's Vitaliani frescoes. This view is rejected by Salmi (*Paolo Uccello, Andrea del Castagno, Domenico Veneziano*, 1938, p. 27–8) on the ground that the frescoes were executed probably in 1445, while the chronicle of Leonardo da Besozzo appears to date from 1436–42. A more fruitful line of research is pursued by Ragghianti ('Casa Vitaliani', in *La Critica d'Arte*, ii, 1938, p. 236 ff.), who seeks for reflections of Uccello's style in the Ovetari Chapel. If the gigantic heads of Pizzolo (Fig. XLIV) and Mantegna on the triumphal arch of the apse of the chapel derive from the Vitaliani 'Giants', these must have been executed in the style of the gigantic heads on the clock-face of the Duomo.

SOURCES OF THE PHOTOGRAPHS

BOSTON
Gardner Museum: Fig. XIII
Museum of Fine Arts: Fig. 18

DUBLIN
National Gallery of Ireland: Fig. XXIV

FLORENCE
Alinari: Pls. 93, 97, 98; Figs. 1, 5, 14, 16, XVII–XIX,
   XXI–XXIII, XXXVI
Brogi: Figs. 1, 11, XX
Conte Alessandro Contini-Bonacossi: Fig. XXV
Scala: Pls. 40, 68, 100
Soprintendenza alle Gallerie: Pls. 1–39, 41–8, 50,
   61–7, 83–92, 95–6, 99; Figs. XXVI–XXVIII,
   XXXVII, XXXVIII, XXXIX

KARLSRUHE
Staatliche Kunsthalle: Fig. XXIX

LONDON
Cooper: Fig. XIV
National Gallery: Pls. 51–60, 78, 80–2; Figs. 7, X
Victoria & Albert Museum: Fig. 17
John R. Freeman: Frontispiece, Pls. 82, 106

LUGANO
Baron H. H. Thyssen-Bornemisza: Fig. XXXIII

NEW YORK
Duveen Bros. Inc.: Fig. IX
Lehman Collection: Fig. XI
Metropolitan Museum: Fig. XII

OXFORD
Ashmolean Museum, Pls. 101–5

PARIS
Agraci: Pl. 77
Giraudon: Pls. 49, 71–4, 79, 107–12
Louvre: Pls. 75–6

PARMA
Soprintendenza alle Gallerie: Fig. XXXV

ROME
Anderson: Fig. XLIV

STOCKHOLM
National Museum: Fig. XLII

VENICE
Soprintendenza ai Monumenti: Fig. XXXVI

VIENNA
Frankenstein: Figs. XL, XLI

WASHINGTON
National Gallery of Art: Figs. VII, VIII, XXXI

INDEX OF PLACES

182

Index of Places

INDEX OF NAMES

Index of Names